Schuetzen Rifles
History and Loadings

by
Gerald O. Kelver

Illustrated with Historical Photographs

3rd Edition ©
Pioneer Press,
Union City, TN
1998

FOREWORD

Since compiling and editing the material for *Major Ned H. Roberts and the Schuetzen Rifle* which was published in 1951, I have had many inquiries regarding the Schuetzen Societies and the very fine single shot rifles used by the old time shooters. Modern day shooters still have an interest in these old guns, yet the information about them is scattered and hard to find. In my own case, my files contain letters and information from many of the old time shooters and the men who made these old time rifles of precision. I became very interested in the Schuetzen rifles when I was young and many of these old timers were still around to answer my numerous questions and to supply information which would have been lost.

Today I am pleased to see a mild revival in the shooting of the fine old single shot rifles of yesterday as well as a keen interest in the collecting and preserving of these rifles.

For myself, I am not partial to factory made guns for it was not, generally speaking, the factory made rifles which established the fine scores made by the good shooters., Rather, it was the rifle which was modified and changed by the specialist who was equipped to meet the shooters' needs. Sometime, because of the press of time some of the work by some of the finest craftsmen may show lack of finish, but the precision of the part was what counted when scores and money were involved.

Factory rifles were custom made and fitted to the shooters' need and pocketbook; therefore, these rifles which were really used could never be classed as standard models although the rifles may have been built on a basic standard production action.

It is my sincere hope that this volume will answer a need of the shooter or collector of the single shot rifle and that true enjoyment will be found in target shooting as in the years past.

Gerald O. Kelver

ACKNOWLEDGEMENTS

PHOTOGRAPHS:

A. W. Peterson, H.M. Pope. National Rifle Association, Washington, D. C.

Southern Ute Indians, J. P. Lower, 4 man Schuetzen Club, State Historical Society, Denver, Colorado.

A. O. Zischang Sharps Borchardt rifles. Abel Merchant, Nassau, New York (Deceased).

George C. Schoyen. John Dutcher, Denver, Colorado.

1878 Sharps A. O. Zischang .32/40, Sharps Borchardt, Freund Boss Gun. Frank Sellers, Denver, Colorado.

1950 American Single Shot Rifle Association Rifle Match. Rupert Hill, Elkhart, Indiana.

All other photographs from author's file.

ACADEMIC ASSISTANCE:

Arapahoe Regional Library, Littleton, Colorado.

Public Library, Worcester, Massachusetts.

Library, State Historical Society of Colorado, Denver, Colorado.

Public Library, Boston, Massachusetts.

Public Library, Western History Department, Denver, Colorado.

Assistance in compiling the material into a presentable form, my wife Ann E. Kelver, Director of Arapahoe Regional Library, Littleton, Colorado.

TABLE OF CONTENTS

CHAPTER   **PAGE**

Chapter 1

EARLY DAYS OF THE SINGLE SHOT RIFLE

The early days of the National Rifle Association are closely tied to the history of the single shot rifles. The National Rifle Association was formed November 21, 1871 with General George W. Wingate as its secretary. General Wingate had been concerned because of the lack of marksmanship and the ignorance of guns manifested during the Civil War by the soldiers. It was his intent as well as the other officers of the Association to instigate and encourage military-type marksmanship. Through the cooperation of the legislature of the state of New York a range was purchased which became known as "Creedmoor." The original targets were imported from England. These targets were made of iron and when hit by a bullet would ring out so that all would know.

Creedmoor was formally opened on June 21, 1872 with teams from several states' National Guards and two Regular Army teams. The Regulars placed last, not knowing how to adjust their sights and knowing nothing of the trajectory of their bullets. These N.R.A. matches were for the purpose of encouraging shooting with military rifles.

The Amateur Rifle Club was organized for the purpose of offhand shooting and long range firing. This was a small club, but most of the members were to become well known as a result of their shooting efforts. General Wingate was elected president of this club.

For some years the English had been holding matches for an award called the Elcho shield. The teams were made up of eight men each from England, Ireland, and Scotland. The ranges at which these teams fired were 800, 900, and 1,000 yards.

In 1873 the Irish won the Elcho shield match and in their exuberance they issued a challenge to the Americans for a world championship match. The Amateur Rifle Club of the United States accepted the challenge in February, 1874. At this time the club consisted of 62 men, and none had ever shot beyond 500 yards.

Considering their own lack of training, of suitable equipment, and no financial means to meet the costs of such an important event they really were amateurs. However, the Remington Arms Company and the Sharps Rifle Company each put up $500 toward a prize and agreed to manufacture a suitable breechloading long range rifle for the team.

At this point national pride had become an issue and

national interest was created since the match would pit the muzzle loaders of the European team against the breech loaders of the Americans.

Both Remington and Sharps made good on their promises, and the rifles were delivered. The caliber of the guns was a .44 caliber, carrying 550 grain bullets, paper patched, and loaded with 75-90 grains of black powder. The cartridge was a bottle neck type, and the groove diameter of the rifles proved to be .452. These rifles were the famous Sharps and Remingtons named after the range where the match was to occur-Creedmoor. Both rifles required a wiping out after each shot through the 34 inch barrels. The sights were long range vernier peep sights and windgauge front sights. These sights were copied from the best of the English long range sights.

General Wingate took over the role of team coach, and for the first time introduced the idea of team sight adjustment so that each man benefited from the sight changes of his predecessor. The Irish, however, fired their matches as individuals composing a team so did not take advantage of this knowledge.

The match was fired on September 26, 1874 which was a hot dry day, but one which was to make the United States marksmanship conscious for the first time. The Americans led by 9 points at 800 yards; at 900 yards it was 7; and at this point the telegraph heralded the news to the world and the range became crowded with over 5,000 spectators.

The Irish finished firing at 1,000 yards first, and as the last American lay down to fire the suspense caused the crowd to ignore safety and pressed in upon the shooter, leaving a narrow V shape down which he had to shoot. The last man to shoot for the Americans was Colonel Bodine who shot from the prone position favored today with the head toward the target. Bodine was the only member of either team to fire in this manner; the rest fired from the reclining position with feet toward the target. This is the reason for the long range sight mounted on the heel of the stock.

Under such exciting circumstances it was necessary to have someone who was not only steady but not subject to excitement from the crowd. The score now was Irish 931, and the Americans 930. A few moments before he was to fire Colonel Bodine had picked up a ginger ale bottle which apparently had been shaken too hard, and as he picked it up the bottle exploded in his hand. Despite the dripping blood, he calmly took his place on the firing point, took a long steady aim and fired. The spat of the bullet on the iron told the story, and the sighting disc at the butts signaled a bullseye, and the American team had won.

The results of this historic match were many. For one thing, it established the breech loading system with its accuracy and more efficient loading. Secondly, it caused the Army to re-evaluate its marksmanship program and to make marksmanship an important part of the training of the soldier. Thirdly, it caused the American public to become aware of recreational shooting.

In the 1874 match all the team members except L. L. Hepburn, the designer of the new Remington Rolling Block Creedmoor, fired Sharps long range rifles. By 1876 the Remington had been so improved that only one man on the U.S. team used a Sharps, and that was Colonel H. A. Gildersleeve. Colonel Bodine, who was honored in 1874 by having the Sharps named "Old Reliable" after him, even forsook the Sharps for the Remington.

In 1875 the Americans again won at Dollymount, Ireland, 967 to 927. In 1876 at Creedmoor the Americans again won over the Irish, Scots, Australians, and Canadians. This match was keenly watched by the whole world, and this centennial celebration of the U. S. added to the prestige of a nation only 100 years old. This was probably the most important rifle match ever sponsored by the National Rifle Association. In a few years we shall be having our second hundred years to celebrate, and the pendulum of public opinion has swung from the glorification and honor of shooting as a sport to total discreditation and an attempt to destroy all the past as irrelevant.

In a subsequent year, 1877, the Americans again won at Creedmoor, and in 1880 shot at Dollymount, Ireland, with the finest shooting that had been done to that point and perhaps ever. Out of 270 shots, 221 were bullseyes; 41 centers; seven inners; one outer; and no misses. This was to be the last international match with the long range match rifles. These beautifully made rifles enjoyed but a brief span of 6 years, and although they were manufactured on special order, there couldn't be too many around for they were very expensive guns in a day when a dollar was worth considerably more than it is today.

In 1880 a new governor of New York was elected who was antagonistic to the National Guard training and claimed it was a waste of time and money. The governor, Alonzo B. Cornell, felt that clubs were of more value to the Guard since they could use them without training. As a result of Governor Cornell's harassment the support the Association had received at Creedmoor was withdrawn, and at the same time the Regular Army which had finally won the Hilton Trophy withdrew its teams from competition. These separate actions, together with the public opinions expressed by the obviously miffed English shooters, caused the civilian long range shooting to be dropped.

At this point small shooting clubs in various parts of the country began to adopt the guns and the type of shooting of the German and Swiss emigrants, and for the first time a new type of rifle was introduced to the American scene and one which we are most concerned about here. This was the single shot target rifle known as the "Schuetzen."

The Schuetzen Rifle made use of much milder cartridges than the long range rifles, the most popular being the .38/55/ 255 and the .32/40/185. In contrast, the Sharps long range guns were made in .40/90/370 straight and bottle necked .44/90/500, .44/105/520, .45/70/420, .45/100/550, and the .45/100/475. In Sharps cartridges these bullets were all paper patched. The Remingtons, Sharps, and early Ballards all had very shallow rifling so that the paper patch could be used. Too deep rifling would cut the patch and eliminate its gas sealing qualities. The Ballard rifle had deeper rifling than the other two and is more suitable for lubricated lead bullets.

In match firing the Sharps Borchardt or hammerless model was the only rifle which proved the equal of the Rigby long range rifles.

Ballard came out with an A1 long range rifle in 1876 in caliber .44/100 Everlasting 2⅝" case and a 2 13/16" case in the hope that it would be used by some of the match shooters, but no one ever adopted it, and this may account for its scarcity at the present time. Later a long range Ballard 7A and 7A1 Extra were used by some shooters, but these rifles were strictly a deluxe custom made rifle.

The "What Cheer" Peabody Martini rifles made by the Providence Tool Co. of Providence, Rhode Island, were introduced in 1880, but too late for the acceptance by shooters in the U.S. although they were used by English shooters at Wimbledon. The rifles were named after the Providence, Rhode Island rifle range rather than Creedmoor which was in New York. The Peabody Martinis were chambered for the .40/70/380, .40/90/500, and the .44/95/550.

Another rifle introduced about the same time but destined for a short life was that manufactured by Frank Wesson of Worcester, Massachusetts. This rifle was called "Creedmoor" and was chambered for the .42/77/730, .44/90/470 Russian, .44/90/500, and .45/100/500.

All of the rifles of that time used a Berdan Primer which long since has been discontinued although RWS, a German company, still makes primers which can be used in these old cases. Brass that is old is brittle and crumbles easily, and to shoot these old cartridges is not advisable. If you shoot one and the head blows off, as it has for me, your trip to the hospital emergency ward is not worth it. If you cannot make the case from a modern brass one, turn or have a machinist turn these cases for you from good brass stock; several cases will be the equal of everlasting cases and will probably last as long as you wish to shoot.

John P. Lower of Denver, Colorado with a Sharps military .45/70/500 Model 1878 and his target of 50 consecutive offhand shots at 200 yards. Fired January 2, 1882.

Chapter 2
THE QUEST FOR ACCURACY

In 1951 a target with a group of ten shots was re-measured, and after fifty years it was confirmed as a measured .725. What rifle and who was the man? The rifle was a Pope Ballard in .32/40, muzzleloaded, using a 200 grain Pope bullet cast 1 part tin to 30 of lead with Leopold lubricant, and using Hazard Black FG powder. The man was C. W. Rowland of Boulder, Colorado, a shooter of the old school. The target was fired in 1901, and the range was 200 yards.

On March 17, 1907 R. Gute, using a Pope Stevens rifle with a Stevens telescope and using Winchester .22 short rimfire ammunition, fired one hundred shots offhand for a score of 2469 out of a possible 2500. While perhaps better scores have been made by others, it would be difficult to find shooters today who could equal the score. Yet, it is not the rifles but the capability of the shooter that limits the score. True, to many of us, a modern free rifle is a far cry from the Stevens Pope or the graceful lines of a Ballard, but yet the guns are being produced which could give outstanding results if the individual practiced as much as the old time Schuetzen shooters and used the same care in his firing. The free rifle, whether Schuetzen or modern, is a heavy rifle well balanced with a tendency to be muzzle heavy. The pronged butt plate, the palm rest, the set triggers are all accessories designed to get the most out of the gun and to enable the shooter to take the same position each time.

The free rifle type of match shooting is credited to Highland, Illinois, when a group of Swiss immigrants in 1853 formed a shooting society patterned on the shooting societies of their native Switzerland. The range was 200 yards, and construction was begun in 1853, finished in 1854. Matches were started in April of that year and were scheduled on Sundays so that the working men could participate. The society was chartered by the State of Illinois and was incorporated. This society was given 31 acres with the provision that should the society disband, the land was to revert to the city.

From 1850 to 1915 Schuetzen clubs were established in many communities where there were Swiss or German settlers, and in Wisconsin such an organization would be found in almost every town. Des Moines and Davenport, Iowa, as well as Denver, Colorado were also well known clubs and there were many others. These clubs were all members of the North American Schuetzen Bund.

4 members of a Schuetzenverein Club in Central Colorado, late 1890's
or early 1900's. Man on left has a Ballard, double set trigger Schuetzen
rifle. 2nd from left has a Ballard with a very unusual offset stock for
shooting righthanded while sighting with left eye. 3rd from left appears
to have a Stevens. The man on far right has a Schoyen double set trigger
engraved Stevens.

The first tournament was at Highland, Illinois, and ran for four days - May 28 through May 31, 1865. Prizes were really prizes, for as much as $5,000 in value was offered. Another aspect of these tournaments was the enormous amount of fine German foods which could be purchased as well as enormous amounts of beer. In 1896 the North American Shooting Bund was reorganized into the Central Sharpshooters Union of North America. (I remember that A. O. Niedner, the famous riflemaker and rifleman of Dowagiac, Michigan, had one of the certificates issued by the Sharpshooters Union for his match work.)

After the start of World War I these Bunds or shooting organizations were looked upon with disfavor, and the membership dropped although efforts were made to keep it alive with .22 rimfire shooting. The last match was held in Davenport, Iowa in 1941.

In 1947 after returning from service in World War II, I met with a group of fellow shooters at Friendship, Indiana, at the National Muzzle Loading Matches and we discussed the necessity for keeping alive the shooting of these fine old single shot rifles. Since I was willing to take on the work of organizing the group, I became Secretary of the American Single Shot Rifle Association and our type of shooting was again on its way. Those who were a part of that first group were B. M. Baxter, John Amber, Bill McCoy, Guy Burch, Rupert Hill, Fred Norton, Joe Whalen, myself, and several others. From this small beginning the Single Shot Rifle Assoication has grown, and each year has seen an increasing number of shooters enter the postal matches as well as the shoulder to shoulder matches first held at Warsaw, Indiana and at Michigan City, Indiana. It is hoped that as interest rises again that other local clubs across the country will revive this pleasant and rewarding type of shooting.

In the old Schuetzen game, offhand was the only position allowed but now the bench type shooting has also been added. Dr. W. G. Hudson, one of the oldtimers of the Colorado Rifle Club, made a world's record offhand at 200 yards which still stands. His record was fired on the American target with a score of 992 out of 1,000 in a 100 shot match.

Most of the records of the Schuetzen days were made with breech loading guns loaded from the muzzle. That is, the bullet was pushed down the barrel from the muzzle end. Muzzle loaders went out with the 1874 matches, yet breech loaders continued to have the bullet seated from the muzzle. Harry Pope's statement on this was as follows, "when a bullet is seated

in the breech, the lands cut into the bullet and push a small
amount of burr to the rear which leaves an uneven base." Unless the bullet is perfectly centered (almost impossible) in the
bore, the burrs are longer on one side than the other. The
gas tends to escape first on the side with the shorter burrs and
this in turn tends to tip the bullet.

Dr. Franklin Mann in his experiments during the time he
was compiling information for the book *The Bullet's Flight*
proved this by distorting the point ends of bullets with relatively
little inaccuracy, but when the bases of the bullets were distorted
by as much as a little nick the flight of the bullet was affected.
Both H. M. Pope and A. O. Niedner worked with Dr. Mann
on these experiments and both were of the same opinion.
Protecting the base of cast bullets is most important. If a bullet
is pushed down the bore from the muzzle any burrs are pushed
forward, and no deforming of the base occurs; also the long
line of the bore provides a means for exact seating.

Oddly enough muzzle loaded bullets seem to need more
"upsetting" than bullets loaded from the breech, so the best
load to use with a rifle used in this manner is a smokeless primer
charge of not over 10% of the whole charge (in .32/40 use 3
to 4 grains BULK of #4227 Dupont powder and the rest of
the case filled with FFG black powder.) Hercules #2400 can
also be used. This load shoots much more cleanly than a full
black powder load and eliminates much of the black powder
fouling of the bore. This load seems to impart a sledge hammer effect to the base of the bullet and seals the gases.

A breech seated bullet, one pushed into the barrel 1/64"
and not over 1/16" ahead of the case (if the barrel is throated
for that bullet), will fire best with regular mild smokeless
loads of Dupont #4227, Unique, #2400, and several others.
These loads are straight loads with no black powder. Do not
try for speed, but rather the lowest load giving the best accuracy.

American Single Shot Rifle Association spring shoot 1950, Warsaw, Indiana. Left to right, Fred Norton, Rupert Hill, A. B. Curtis, Bill McCoy. Rear, left to right, G. O. Kelver, Anthony Whalen, Joseph Whalen.

Chapter 3

NEWS ITEMS AND SCORES FROM OLD JOURNALS

Old time sporting newspapers and magazines were not hesitant about printing endorsements or criticisms of any make of rifle. Some of the letters are quite amusing; many have bits of information we can find nowhere else; and some are down right critical.

American Field, February 27, 1886.

"I would say that the shooting club of Lagrange, Wisconsin, consider the 32-40 Ballard equal to any single shot rifle made in the United States. In a shoot held near this place this winter and where there were but eight turkeys in all to shoot for, the little 32-40 Ballard carried off or won them all, and this, too, against muzzle and breech rifles, distance 330 yards. The other rifles competing were .38/21, .40/60, and .40/75. After this shoot the boys had a turkey shoot to give those who had heavy guns a chance to outshoot the little gun, if they could, distance 385 yards, but in this, as in all other previous matches, it came out ahead, beating the next best gun on the ground two to one. The gun is all right in every respect.

Badger

American Field, January 16, 1886.

"The Best Rifle for Two Hundred Yards"

New York City, Editor American Field: In reply to Mr. Dibble's communication regarding the best rifle for 200 yard work. I can recommend the Maynard as the thing for all around work. It possesses one great advantage over all other rifles in the interchanging of barrels which can be done while using one of the same stock. I have owned rifles of nearly all the leading makes and I never owned anything that could excel my Maynard, or rather Maynards, for I own two barrels - a .22 caliber, 10 grain and a .35 caliber, 40 grain. The .35 caliber barrel is 28 inches long while my .22 caliber is only 24 inches. I use both the Lyman rear sight and the Beach front sight. There are other sights which may excel these but for general use I prefer these. For 200 yard rifle shooting I would recommend either the .32 caliber or .35 caliber Maynard, although my little .22 caliber can show a good record at 200 yards the shell for this little weapon being especially adapted for this kind of work. I enclose a target made at seventy-five feet with my .22 caliber Maynard. I did not finish the target as you will see only nine shots are noted, being called away just as I was going to fire the tenth. I am not an expert, far from it, but

I am an enthusiast on the shooting qualities of the Maynard and speak a good word for it on every possible occasion.

.35 Caliber

The above letter is certainly enthusiastic, but leads to many doubts. If you read it carefully you will find some amusing contradictions and an alibi that would do the modern shooter credit. The .22 the writer speaks of is not the .22 long rifle rimfire, for this cartridge had not even been developed, but rather a little straight cased center fire cartridge developed by Maynard.

Sometimes as we read about scores made in the good old days and how accurately these old single shot rifles shot, we wonder just how accurate they were. With this thought in mind I decided to include a few of these scores as reported by the secretaries of the various clubs so that we can really judge the question of accuracy for ourselves. The following was reported in the *American Field* March 13, 1886.

Rifle at Rawlins, Wyo. The following is the score of the Capital City Rod and Gun Club at its regular shoot held Saturday, February 27. The day was fearfully cold and very windy. Conditions two hundred yards, offhand, open sights, American Field Target.

Last Name	Rifle	Caliber	Score					Total
Mathews	Sharps	40-70	1	3	2	4	2	12
Smith	Winchester	45-60	0	3	3	0	0	6
Daley	Remington	40-65	3	0	2	3	2	10
Inglis	Sharps	40-70	3	5	4	6	1	19
Glenn	Winchester	45-60	1	10	0	0	0	11
Johnson	Remington	40-65	2	1	0	2	0	5
Reid	Winchester	45-60	4	3	2	5	0	14
Thompson	Winchester	45-60	2	0	2	7	0	11
Blydenburg	Bullard	40-75	6	6	8	4	4	28
O'Melia	Ballard	45-70	2	2	3	1	0	8
McCarty	Winchester	45-60	2	2	3	0	2	9
Hill	Remington	40-65	7	3	5	8	2	25

In the same issue another item of interest appears under Colorado Rifle Notes, Leadville, Colo. "The Schuetzen Verein which was organized here is still flourishing. Practice shots were held throughout the summer months and occasionally there was a prize shoot. I admit we cannot compete with America's International Team but I notice some scores in the American Field much lower than ours. The gun we use is Sharps Model of 1878 (hammerless) and we are not allowed to use globe or peep sights. Our range is 200 yards and all shooting is done offhand.

Wild Hack

Also March 13, 1886, the following appeared:
Scores for the two top shooters at Battleboro, Vt. 200 yards offhand, Hinman target were:

| W. M. Farrow | 7 | 8 | 10 | 8 | 10 | 7 | 9 | 8 | 8 | 10 - 85 |
| G. B. Read | 9 | 7 | 10 | 8 | 8 | 10 | 10 | 7 | 9 | 7 - 85 |

February 20, 1886 - 10 shots offhand, 200 yards, no sighters.

| W. M. Farrow | 10 | 7 | 7 | 8 | 10 | 7 | 8 | 7 | 9 | 9 - 82 |
| A. S. Nichols | 10 | 8 | 9 | 7 | 8 | 6 | 6 | 6 | 9 | 10 - 79 |

Team Practice scores:

| W. M. Farrow | 9 | 10 | 8 | 6 | 10 | 10 | 9 | 10 | 10 | 7 - 89 |
| C. L. Cobb | 6 | 10 | 7 | 6 | 7 | 10 | 8 | 10 | 9 | 7 - 80 |

American Field, March 27, 1886.

"Rifle at Pittsburgh - The weather was again unfavorable for shooting, although it was an improvement on the bothersome wind of February 18. Mr. L. Brehm used a .32/40/180 Ballard rifle for the first time and seemed well pleased with its performance, although he believes his long range Sharps, with a special charge of 55 grains of powder and 420 grains of lead is more reliable in windy weather. On March 4 the following scores were made: (Hinman target, 200 yards offhand)

L. Brehm, Ballard	.32/40/180 grooved	73 70 77 72 79
G. Hodgdon, Remington	.32/20/120 grooved	77 65 70 71 66
F. Stolle, Ballard	.38/50/330 grooved	70 75 73 69 79

In the same issue it was noted in the Springfield, Massachusetts Club Notes that the high composite score at 200 yards offhand on the Hinman target was by E. T. Stephens with a 79. J. Allen was last with a 72 and one his eighth shot he drew a blank. The footnote says "J. Allen forgot to put a bullet in his gun."

American Field, March 20, 1886.

"Rifle at Chicopee Falls, Mass. - The Maynard Rifle Club had a nice afternoon for its practice shoot on March 6. The shooting was fairly good. Hinman target, 200 yards offhand:

R. Garden, Maynard .35 7 8 9 9 7 8 7 8 5 9   77
    45 grs. powder, 240
    grs. lead, patched
W. Ellsworth, Stevens .22 8 10 6 4 6 10 7 9 9 6   75
    10 grs. powder, 65 grs.

lead, grooved
A. Clark, Horr .22	8	4	10	8	8	7	7	7	8	5	72

10 grs. powder, 65 grs.
lead, grooved
H. Engle, Stevens .32	7	7	10	10	6	5	4	6	7		72

35 grs. powder, 165 grs.
lead, patched
C. W. Horr, Horr .22	6	5	8	8	7	6	7	5	7	10	69

10 grs. powder, 65 grs.
lead, grooved
Brooks, Maynard .38	10	8	8	5	8	5	9	0	7	6	66

45 grs. powder, 255 grs.
lead, patched

American Field, June 19,1886.
"The spring meeting of the Peekskill, N. Y. National Rifle Club for 1886 came off as published on May 26 and 27. The weather was cold.
Breech Loaders

I. N. Frye	10 lbs.	Ballard	.38 cal.	held to shoulder
G. F. Ellsworth	10 lbs.	Ballard	.38 cal.	held to shoulder
F. J. Rabbeth	10 lbs.	Remington	.38 cal.	held to shoulder
C. W. Hinman	10 lbs.	Maynard	.35 cal.	held to shoulder
W. M. Farrow	9 lbs.	Farrow	.32 cal.	double fixed rest."

American Field, March 27, 1886.
"Rifle at Fairmont, Minn. - On March 11, E. W. Bird took out a new Winchester single shot .32/40 which he had just received from the factory, it never having been fired before. It took three shots to find the target. The first twenty five shots counting the first one that found the target, were as follows, 200 yards offhand, Hinman target:

E. W. Bird	4	8	7	7	8	6	9	9	8	9	78
	5	8	10	6	8	10	8	7	7	6	75
	9	8	6	8	6						37
J. W. Bird	7	9	7	9	6	5	9	10	7	10	79
.32/40 Bal.											

On March 13 the following scores were made at 500 yards:

E. W. Bird	4	5	4	5	4	4	5	5	5	5	46
Springfield Mil.											

J. W. Bird	5	5	5	3	5	5	5	5	3	4	45
.32/40 Bal.											

Heel Plate"

American Field, April 24, 1886.

"- I have never seen the Winchester single shot rifle, and have no doubt it is first class in every respect, but I will guarantee that either a Maynard, a Remington, a Ballard, or a Bullard is as finely adjusted as the riflemen of this country require.

A string of ten shots was fired a few days ago on the range of the Norwalk Rifle Club, 200 yards offhand, and seven were inside a six inch circle. This was done with a Ballard rifle.

Fritz"

American Field, January 22, 1881.

"Boston, Mass., January 9. The closing day of the several matches, brought to the Walnut Hill Range a very large number of riflemen who did some excellent shooting. The following scores will show what the amateurs did:

E. J. Cram	5	4	5	5	4	4	5	5	5	5 - 47
A. C. Gould	5	5	5	4	5	4	4	5	5	5 - 47
C. H. Grant	5	5	5	5	5	4	4	4	4	5 - 46

Massachusetts target, 200 yards offhand. Cram - Gold Medal, Gould - Silver Medal.

Ranger"

Walnut Hill, the famous rifle range located in Massachusetts, is described in a very fine article which appeared January 22, 1881 in the *Chicago Field,* as follows:

"Boston Riflemen and Ranges

Editor Chicago Field:—As the Chicago Field has more readers in Boston than any other sporting paper published, and as our riflemen and rifle ranges are a prominent feature of our legitimate sports, I this week add to my usual report of matches and range practice, a short synopsis of who our best marksmen are, and where the ranges are situated, and how a stranger can reach them on starting from Boston. The central point, the first of which I will take up, is the Walnut Hill Range.

The range of the Massachusetts Rifle Association is located in the eastern part of Woburn "The Walnut Hill district," ten and one-half miles from Boston, on the Boston and Lowell railroad, and one-half mile from the Walnut Hill Station. The fare from Boston for a single ticket is sixty cents round trip, but the association have special commutation tickets, issued only to members of the Massachusetts Rifle Association, for ten rides between Boston and Walnut Hill for one dollar and twenty-five cents. Passengers can also take conveyance between the Walnut Hill Station and the range by barge, of which Mr. William Kendall is proprietor of the best: fare ten cents each way.

The range contains about forty acres of land, which is divided into ranges of from 200 yards to 1100 yards distances.

Upon the grounds are two buildings, the lower one in the rear of the 1000 yards firing points, and the Pavilion on the 200 yards firing points. In the Summer time the latter can be opened all around by raising the sides, and in the Winter it is kept closed, and heated by two large stoves. In front of this building will be seen six targets, four of iron, and two of paper, on a sash of canvas. The former are divided for Creedmoor count, the latter for Massachusetts count. The scores on the latter are indicated on a large clock-face at the right of each target. Beneath these targets is a pit, heated by a stove, where the markers stay during shooting. It is protected from the bullets by an embankment of earth about ten feet thick. These targets are four by six feet and used for all distances up to and including 300 yards, bull's-eye eight inches in diameter. Farther down the range will be seen two more targets of iron, size six by six feet, bull's-eye twenty-two inches in diameter, used for all distances over 300 yards up to and including 600 yards. The body of the range is used for the long range, for which there are four targets, size six by twelve feet and used for all distances from 600 up to and including 1100 yards. Making a total of twelve targets in all, at which a very large number of riflemen can be accommodated at the same time.

There will also be seen upon the range four large red flags on poles about forty feet high; used to denote the direction of the wind as is also the large clock or dial which is in full view of all ranges or distances. Also at each firing point will be seen small red flags which are used as signals to the markers.

At the entrance and upon the Pavilion two United States flags float proudly in the breeze. The 200-yards' pit is connected with the Pavilion by telephone, which is very convenient. In this pavilion at about noon time will be seen a large table spread with delicacies agreeable to the educated appetites of the riflemen. Spectators also can get a good dinner for a moderate price, furnished by the caterer, Mr. William Kendall.

This range held its formal opening on Thursday, November 16, 1876, having only two targets and those on the 200-yards' range. There were only thirty members who indulged in the pool and prize shooting. The first prize, the bronze medal of the National Rifle Association, was won by Mr. J. B. Osborn, and the four other prizes were won by Messrs. Sanborn, Poland, Rockwell and Osgood. The range was laid out and superintended by Capt. W. H. Jackson, who from the beginning has been a very active member upon the range.

Among the riflemen will be found some very excellent marksmen. So many of them are excellent shots their names would be "too numerous to mention." Mr. J. N. Frye, now president of the association, is always present at all matches extending a welcome and friendly hand to all visitors, as well as to his brother sportsmen.

Mr. George Fowle has been the range keeper since the opening, but he is getting quite aged now, is wearing out faster than the iron targets and some of the young members, and will soon have to resign his position.

The Massachusetts Rifle Association now includes upward of 200 members and is in a healthy, growing and prosperous condition.

In some future number I will give you a description of some of the other Boston ranges.

Ranger"

In the *American Field* of February 27, 1886 a writer comments on the Bullard rifle:

"The Bullard Single-Shot Rifle.—Worcester, Mass. Editor American Field:—A short time ago I noticed several inquiries about the Bullard Single-shot rifle, and, as I purchased one of the first the company got out, I shall give my opinion. It is a .35-caliber and I must say it does the best shooting of any rifle I ever owned, and I have owned and shot every kind of rifle made in this part of the country. My first trial was made at the Manchester Fall meeting, before which time I had shot only seven shots from the rifle. The totals given are for strings of ten shots each on the Massachusetts target, and are as follows: 83, 82 and 86. At Walnut Hill, on October 11, shooting at the same target, strings of seven shots each, I made totals of 60 and 63. Again, At Walnut Hill, on January 30, shooting at the Hinman target, strings of ten shots, I made totals of 88, 83 and 87. These scores will prove to your correspondent the accuracy of this new Bullard rifle.

A. C. White"

Chapter 4

A SHORT HISTORY

OF THE STEVENS ARMS COMPANY

The story of the Stevens must of necessity begin with the founder of the company that was to become known as the one which produced the world's most accurate rifles as well as the most popular.

Joshua Stevens was born in Chelsea, Massachusetts in 1814. By 1834 he was a machinist's apprentice, and in 1838 he went to work for Cyrus B. Allen in Springfield, Massachusetts. Sometime after 1838 Stevens went to work for Samuel Colt at the Colt factory in Hartford, Connecticut. Stevens, in association with two other machinists, subcontracted work on the Colt revolvers at the Colt factory. There was some type of disagreement, and Stevens was discharged and the contract terminated.

Joshua Stevens then went to work for Edwin Wesson who, at the time, was working on a revolver design which he had patented. Shortly after Stevens began working for Wesson, Wesson died. Stevens continued to work on the pistol and received a patent for a minor change in the locking system.

In 1849 Joshua Stevens moved to Chicopee Falls, Massachusetts and began to work for the Massachusetts Arms Company which was formed in December, 1849. This company had in turn purchased the shop from the Ames Manufacturing Company for the purpose of manufacturing firearms, sewing machines, and other machinery. Stevens apparently was employed to help in designing products for the new company.

Based on the Edwin Wesson revolver, which Stevens had received patents on for a cylinder stop, the Massachusetts Arms Company began the manufacture of the "Stevens" revolver. Colt sued the Massachusetts Arms Company for a patent infringement and Colt won. The Massachusetts Arms Company was forced to pay $15,000 to Colt, an amount they could ill afford. Later they recouped their loss through purchasing the rights to manufacture the Maynard rifle.

Joshua Stevens continued in his employment with the Massachusetts Arms Company until 1864. In 1864 the Stevens Arms Company was formed by three partners who were later to play prominent parts in the corporation of later years. The listed partners were Joshua Stevens, James E. Taylor, and William B. Fay. By 1867 the company was employing 30 men in the manufacture of firearms and machinists' tools. The name of this company was officially known as the J. Stevens & Company, Chicopee Falls, Massachusetts.

One of the successful products of this new company was the first of the "tip ups", meaning that the whole barrel assembly was pivoted at the front of the action, and the barrel tipped "down" from the action when loading and "up" when returned to firing position. This successful action was first manufactured in a pistol.

In the January 9, 1886 issue of the *American Field* the note appears, "The old and popular firm of J. Stevens   Co. of Chicopee Falls, Mass., manufacturers of the celebrated firearms and fine machinists' tools, have sold out their business to the new business just formed under the name of the J. Stevens Arms & Tool Co. with the following officers: Joshua Stevens, president; William B. Fay, Joshua Stevens, Geo. S. Taylor, directors; Irving H. Page, secretary; James E. Taylor, agent and treasurer. The above took possession of the business January 1, 1886."

From 1875 to 1895 the manufacturing of the Stevens firearms was contained in a three story frame structure. In 1893 William B. Fay, who was one of the original three partners and who had always been the factory manager, died. In December, 1895 Joshua Stevens, who was now 81 years old, retired.

Irving H. Page, who was associated with the business, purchased the interests of Joshua Stevens and James E. Taylor on January 1, 1896. Charles P. Fay, the son of William B. Fay, who had inherited his father's interest, became vice president and general superintendent.

From 1895 the business grew from 44 employees to 900 in 1900. By 1908 Stevens had a total manufacturing floor space of 14 acres and proudly claimed to be the largest producer of sporting firearms in the world. It was also during this period of phenomenal growth that Harry M. Pope, the famous barrel maker, became associated with the company and laid the foundations for the rifle that was known for its accuracy.

Joshua Stevens died in 1907 at the age of ninety-two. He lived a long life and saw the humble beginning of his company grow to one of the largest in the world at that time. Truly a credit to the sound engineering and popular price of a worthy product.

Actually, the tip up pistols manufactured by Stevens may have had their primary beginning in the Maynard rifles of Civil War fame, for they too were "tip up" actions operated by an underlever and permitting the barrel to "tip" down for loading. In fact, the old Maynard Company was bought out by Stevens somewhere around 1884. Advertisements in the *American Field* continued through 1883 in the name of the Massachusetts Arms Company and proudly proclaimed the accuracy and reliability of the Maynard system.

Rifles, pistols, and shotguns were manufactured by Stevens on the tip up action until 1894 when the first Model 44, known as the Ideal, was patented and produced. The 1894 models all have one side of the breech block cut away for the extractor, and the extractor is on the left side of the chamber. This cutting away of the bearing surface of the breech block makes this a considerably weaker action than the later improvement which introduced a solid breech block with a central hung extractor in the lower central part of the chamber.

Either under the influence of H. M. Pope or the company, the Model 44 action was greatly improved by the introduction of a sliding breech block assembly. This improved version became known as the Ideal Model 44½. The 44½ Stevens today is known for its strength, simplicity, and ease of operation.

Between 1867 and 1872 the Stevens Arms Company existed by manufacturing pistols, calipers, dividers, and agriculture or nursery shears. In 1872 the company introduced breech loading shotguns, and the work force grew to forty men. By 1877-78 sporting rifles increased in demand, and the company put on an additional work force.

In 1901 Stevens introduced a line of new conventional shotguns. In 1908 they introduced a shotgun based on a John M. Browning patent. In 1910 they introduced a high power repeating rifle, and this was shown in Catalog #53, dated 1911. The rifles were advertised as being in .25, .30/30, .32, or .35 caliber.

In Catalog #54, dated 1914, they advertised a No. 101 Featherweight 44 gauge shotgun using an action similar to a No. 12 Marksman rifle advertised in the #55 Catalog of December 1, 1920.

Catalog #54 proclaims the fact that "Stevens Firearms have been made and sold for a half century - there are no substitutes."

Stevens manufactured shotguns under the trade name "Riverside Arms Co." from shortly before World War I to about 1928 or 1929. They also manufactured both rifles and shotguns under the trade name "Springfield Arms Co." About 1919 the firm name was changed from the J. Stevens Arms & Tool Company to the J. Stevens Arms Company of Chicopee Falls, Massachusetts. Thus the company had come full cycle back to the beginning name.

In 1915, just one year after their fiftieth year in business, the J. Stevens Arms and Tool Company was acquired by the Westinghouse Electric Company. During World War I the company was used to manufacture firearms and parts for the Allies.

In 1920 the Savage Arms Corporation of Utica, New York purchased the J. Stevens Arms Company. From 1920 to 1946 the plant continued to operate as a subsidiary plant of the Savage Arms Corporation.

As far as rifles are concerned, the Stevens catalogs feature the finest rifles from the time Pope joined the firm in 1901 through Catalog #54 in 1914. From 1914 the catalogs featured fewer rifles and more shotguns. By 1926 Stevens claimed to be the largest shotgun manufacturers in the world.

In 1940 Stevens converted from sporting arms to military production and manufactured the Lee Enfield rifle for British lend lease. Stevens manufactured both Short Lee Enfields and No. 4 Mark I. These Stevens rifles can be identified by an S in front of the model number on the receiver. All these rifles were .303 British caliber, and all went overseas, so any in this country would be few in number.

By 1946-47 commercial sporting firearms were again being manufactured by the Stevens Arms Company. However, a fateful decision had been made, and that was not to manufacture any of the lever action falling block rifles that had proven to be so popular over the past years. With this decision an era passed along with the Schuetzenfests of bygone years.

Chapter 5

EARLY STEVENS RIFLES

Hunters of the 1880's in the Ute Pass area of Colorado. The man on the right has a new tip-up Stevens rifle. Note the unsafe position of his left hand.

The early models are known for their characteristic tip up actions in rifle, shotgun, and pistol. Many refer to these rifle actions as the "Premier" rifles. However, this term refers actually to a particular model number as we shall see. Also, it is to be noted that the actual "Premier" rifles had a wood forend. All parts for Stevens Rifles Nos. 1 to 16 and the "Hunter's Pet" interchanged, so there was little actual difference in the guns.

From the 1898 catalog we find that the Stevens Company believed in a positive approach to th. ˙ ˙ firearms. "In the manufacture of Stevens rifles, we have also borne in mind that a rifle to give valuable service must be strongly and perfectly made and the many testimonials which we receive from thousands of friends who have Stevens rifles in their possession, which they have been using for years and years back still use today with perfect satisfaction, assure us that we have not failed in our endeavors."

"We receive daily rifles to be rebored which have been in use from ten to twenty years and yet the people using them merely need to have the barrel rebored to have a good strong and practically, to them, new rifle. This in itself speaks volumes for the quality and durability of Stevens arms."

Many single shot firearms were rebored from the original shot-out calibers to different ones. These rebores were and are accurate, yet today if a single shot is believed to be a "rebore" it's a dead issue as far as the modern buyer is concerned, for it is not "original." What the term original means in the case of the single shot rifles is rather dubious, but to most collectors it has a magic ring. Factually, what is more original than a rebore by the factory itself?

In 1898 the factory still had on hand tip up actions in Numbers 2, 5, and 7 in .38 rimfire, and in center fire calibers .32 Long, .25-20, .32-35, .32-40, and .38-55 in barrel lengths from 24 inches to 30 inches. It was noted in this special offering that it had been decided not to offer these rifles in these calibers after February 1, 1898 except in the special listing.

The following are the tip up rifles offered by Stevens:

Stevens No. 1 Open Sight Rifles. Full octagon barrel, open sights, nickle plated frame and butt plate, oiled walnut stock. Center fire calibers .32, .38, and .44 as well as rimfire. Barrel lengths were 24, 26, 28, and 30 inches. Weight 6½ to 8¼ pounds. Price $20, $21, $22, 23, depending on the barrel length. No forearm.

Stevens No. 2 Open Sight Rifles. Full octagon barrel, open sights, nickle plated frame and butt plate, oiled walnut stock. .22 Long Rifle R. F., .25 R. F., and .32 Long R. F. With 24 inch barrel only, weight 7 pounds, $17. No forearm.

Stevens No. 3. This rifle was the same as No. 1 except that it had Stevens combination open and peep sights and was offered in either half or full octagonal barrels. Price $23, $24, $25, and $26 depending on the barrel length. The sight was $3 extra. No forearm..

Stevens No. 4 Gallery Rifle. Same as No. 2 but $3 higher for the Stevens combination sight. The caliber was .22 Long Rifle R.F., .25 R.F., and .32 Long R.F. No forearm.

Stevens No. 5 Expert Rifle. Half octagon barrel, Beach combination front sight, open rear sight, and Vernier peep sight (can be changed in an instant from a globe to a plain open sight rifle), varnished stock, nickle plated frame and butt plate. Calibers .22 Long Rifle R.F., .25 R.F., and .32 Long R.F. 24 inch barrel only, weight 6¾ pounds. $20.

Prior to February 1, 1898 the No. 5 was made in barrel lengths 24, 26, 28, and 30 inches. The calibers were .38 R.F., .32 Long C.F., .25/20 C.F., .32-35 C.F., .32-40 C.F., .38-55 C.F. These rifles also were offered in .22 Short R.F., .32, .38, and .44 Long rimfire. In 1898 the prices for the No. 5 were $18, $18.75, $19.50, and $20.

Stevens No. 6 Expert Rifle. Same as No. 5 except with a fancy stock and an increased price. The Numbers 5 and 6 did not have a forearm.

Stevens No. 7 Premier Rifle. Half octagon barrel (front part was round), Beach combination open sight, open rear sight, Vernier peep sight, varnished stock *and forearm,* Swiss butt-plate, frame and butt plate nickle plated. Calibers .22 Long Rifle R.F., .25 R.F., and .32 Long R.F. Barrels 24 inch, 7¾ pounds, and 28 inch, 8¾ pounds. This model was also made in .38 and .44 rim or center fire.

Stevens No. 8 Premier Rifle. Same rifle as Stevens No. 7 but with fancy wood in butt stock and forend. Prices were adjusted for the fancier wood.

Stevens No. 9 New Model Range Rifle. Half octagon barrel, wind gauge front sight, Vernier rear. Varnished stock and forend. Frame nickle plated as was the Schuetzen style butt plate. Calibers .22 Long Rifle R.F. or C.F., .32, .38, and .44 R.F. or C.F. chambered for the .32/35/165 cartridge using patched or grooved bullets. Barrels were 24, 26, 28, and 30 inches with prices according to the barrel length from $31.50 to $37.50.

Stevens No. 10 Range Rifle. Same as Stevens No. 9 but with selected stocks. Chambered for .22 Long rimfire. Also for .22

Extra Long C.F. Maynard. Prices averaged $3.00 higher than the No. 9.

Stevens No. 11, 12, 13, and 14 were classed as "Ladies Rifles." Barrels 24 and 26 inches long half octagon. Calibers .22 R.F. Long and .22 Maynard C.F. Weight 5½ pounds. Varnished stock and forend, sight combination varied from open to Beach front and Vernier rear sights. Prices were from $25 to $30. Action slimmer than the regular and nickle plated. No. 14 and a fancy stock which added $2 to the rifle. The Nos. 11 and 13 were also chambered for the .22 Long Rifle R.F. and .25 R.F.

Stevens Nos. 15 and 16 Crack Shot Rifles. Full octagon barrel, Lyman ivory bead front sight and Lyman's combination rear sight on frame. Nickle plated frame and butt plate (crescent rifle type). Calibers .22 Short R.F., .32, .38, and .44 Long rim or center fire. Oiled stock. Barrels 24, 26, 28, and 30 inches long. Weight from 6½ to 8¼ pounds. Prices $26 to $29. No. 16 was same description as No. 15 but with a fancy stock and a $3 increase in price. The advertisement on on these bore a special note "Center fire rifles chambered to order only."

The following tip ups had a wood forend installed by the factory - Nos. 7 through 14. The rest of the tip up rifles did not have a wood forend, being plain with the barrel underside being used as a hand rest.

For those rifles using the .22 caliber long rimfire cartridges the company had this to offer in 1888:

"Weight of bullet 40 grains. Being 11 grains heavier than the regular .22 Long. These cartridges are made expressly for accurate shooting up to 200 yards in rifles especially adapted to them having increased twist in rifling and manufactured by the Stevens Arms Co. They differ materially from regular .22 Long R. F. cartridges, both as to quantity of powder and weight of bullet. Guns taking this cartridge, will, without cleaning, shoot the hundredth shot as accurately as the first."

One of the early model rifles in especially fine condition examined by the author recently was an Open Sight Rifle, Stevens No. 2. Number 19690 appeared on the lower tang at the rear just in front of lower tang screw. Barrel is marked on left side beginning at the rear sight "J. Stevens & OC, Chicopee Falls, Mass. Pat Sept. 9, 1884" (Note: the "C" in CO reversed as well as the 9 in Sept.) No. 19690 also appears on the breech of the barrel on left side. Caliber is .32 R.F. The firing pin strikes the case on the top edge. The extractor is a sliding extractor operating in the central lower part of the barrel. The lower 3 octagon flats are missing on the lower part of the barrel which extends into the action, this part of the barrel being rounded for 5 inches from the rear of the barrel. The front sight is quite interesting in that it has a pivoted 3 point series of sight choices from a blade to a copper bead to an ivory bead. In the January 9, 1886 issue of *The American Field* the following appears on page 41.

"Richmond, Ind. - I recently made a very good score with a Stevens Premier rifle which I think worth publishing. The rifle was .32 caliber, twenty six inch barrel, loaded with twenty grains of powder. The distance was 200 yards, off hand, on the Massachusetts target. I shot twenty five shots aggregating 262. The total of the first ten shots was 104; the second ten 104, and the last five 54.

C. A. Jackson

Chapter 6

STEVENS SINGLE SHOT RIFLES

OF THE "GOLDEN ERA"

Stevens rifles reached their zenith in the period from 1898 to 1914. It was during this period that the very beautiful and accurate rifles were made which gave Stevens its fame. In the better grades the rifle was made to suit the requirement of the most exacting shooter. Rifles were made plain for the field or elaborate for the offhand and rest target shooter.

A review of the rifles offered in 1911 shows a great variety from the "Little Scout" to the "Schuetzen Special." A listing of these rifles might be helpful to the shooter or collecor.

No. 14½ "Little Scout" - take down .22 caliber, weight 2¾ lbs. List price $2.50. 18 inch round barrel, casehardened frame, blued steel butt plate. Open sight - German silver blade block pyramid rear. Chambered for C.B. caps, .22 short, .22 long, or .22 long rifle rim fire.

No. 15 "Maynard Jr." Weight 2¾ pounds. List price $3.00. Tip down barrel 18 inch half octagon, casehardened frame, blued steel butt plate. German silver blade front, pyramid rear. Chambered for C.B. caps, .22 short, .22 long, or .22 long rifle rim-fire.

No. 15½ "Maynard Jr. Shotgun" same as above except smooth bored for .22 shot cartridge.

No. 16 "Crack Shot" take down .22 C.B. caps, .22 short, .22 long, or .22 long rifle rim-fire. Weight 3¾lbs. 20 inch round barrel, casehardened frame, walnut stock and forend, rubber butt plate, open sights - bead front. List price $4.00.

No. 16½ "Crack Shot Shotgun" same as above but smooth bored for .32 R.F. shot cartridge.

No. 17 "Favorite", half octagon barrel 22, 24, or 26 inches. Frame casehardened, automatic ejector in .22, stock walnut, shotgun butt, rubber butt plate, walnut forend. Open sights. Model No. 1, C.B. caps or .22 short. Model No. 2, C.B. caps, .22 short, .22 long, or .22 long rifle; also .25 long rimfire cartridges. Also special order .22 WRF.

No. 18 - Same as No. 17 except Beach front sight and No. 106 Stevens leaf and vernier tang sight.

No. 19 - Same as No. 17 except fitted with Lyman No. 5 and No. 106 Stevens leaf and Lyman 1A tang sight.

No. 20 "Favorite Shotgun", 22 inch barrel, shotgun front sight. .22 or .32 rimfire shot cartridges. Same as No. 17.

No. 21 "Favorite Ladies Model", take down. Barrel half octagon 24 or 26 inches long. Sights #205 Beach, No. 112 sporting rear, and No. 102 vernier. .22 short, .22 long rifle, .25 Stevens, .32 long. Special order .22 WRF and .22/15/60 C.F. Stock and forearm checkered, butt pistol grip, buttplate #2 Swiss.

No. 44 "Ideal" - take down, barrel number 2 weight only, half octagon 24 inches in rimfire calibers, 26 inches in center fire calibers. Casehardened frame, auto ejector in .22 only. Walnut forend and butt stock, plain. No. 1 steel butt plate. #203 Rocky Mountain front sight and No. 112 sporting rear. .22 short, .22 long rifle, .25 Stevens, and .32 long rimfire cartridges. .25/20 Stevens, .32/20 center fire cartridges. Price $10.00.

No. 44½ "Ideal" - same as No. 44 except offered in additional calibers .32/40, .32 Ideal, and .32 Long center fire. Extra chambering costs for .22 WRF, .22/15/60, .25/25, .28/30/120. Price $12.00.

No. 44½ "Ideal" English Model - same as above except it had a shotgun type butt stock with rubber butt plate. Price $12.00.

No. 45 "Ideal Range" model, offered in No. 2 half octagon 28 inch barrel. No. 2 Swiss butt plate same as 44½ Ideal. #102 vernier tang sight. Price $22.00.

No. 47 "Ideal Modern Range" - same chambering, same specifications as No. 45. Butt stock was plain, pistol grip, No. 2 Swiss butt plate; lever was long loop. Price $29.50.

No. 49 "Ideal Walnut Hill" - same specifications as No. 45. Forend was checkered as was pistol grip. Butt stock with cheek piece and No. 3 Swiss butt plate, loop lever, scroll engraved receiver, windgauge front sight. Price $46.25.

No. 51 "Ideal Schuetzen" - barrel No. 2 or 3 half octagon 30 inches long. Same as No. 49 except for butt stock which had straight grip, cheek piece, and #4 Schuetzen butt plate. Finger lever had finger rest and wood panels in loop. Windgauge front sight. Price $61.50.

No. 52 "Ideal Schuetzen Jr." - same as No. 51 except pistol grip stock and Pope type finger lever. Windgauge front sight. Price $63.50.

No. 54 "Ideal Schuetzen Special" - same as No. 51 except butt plate was #5 and Pope type palm rest. Windgauge front sight. Price $77.00.

No. 56 "Ideal Ladies Model" - barrel half octagon in 24 inches for rimfire and 26 inches for center fire cartridges. Rifle was plain 44½ casehardened. Forend was checkered as was pistol grip butt stock. Butt plate was No. 2 Swiss. Offered in .22 short,

.22 long rifle, .22 WRF, .25 Stevens, and .32 long rimfire cart-ridges. .22/15/60, .25/20 Stevens, 25/21, 25/25, .28/30/120, .32/20 center fire cartridges.

No. 404 "Semi Military Model" - 44 action, round 28 inch barrel, auto ejector, walnut shotgun butt with rubber plate, special extra wide walnut forend 12 inches long. Forend only was checkered. #210 Globe front and #42 Lyman receiver sights. .22 long rifle only. Price $27.00. Had a sling button on barrel, no rear sling swivel.

Stevens also from 1901 to 1914 offered rifle accessories based on H. M. Pope's patents and development. Many of the accessories which shooters find and label as Pope may have actually been madé and furnished by Stevens for their rifles rifles during this period. The accessories are all made to Pope's exacting standards, yet such devices were not made by Pope. These accessories include the double charge Pope powder measure made for duplex loading, Pope's re and de-capper made in all standard calibers, Pope's double cut off molds, and Pope's lubricating pump and dies. The lubricant offered was Leo-pold's formula.

In 1888 through the Stevens-Pope catalog of 1902 the Stevens Company offered to recut barrels, either their own or for rifles of other makes. However, by Catalog Number 53, 1914, this service was no longer offered.

Under the Pope system of rifling, Stevens offered to re-rifle to the following calibers: .25/25, .28/30, .32/40 Marlin, .33 Special, .38/55, .38/72 Special, and to the .39 Special in 1902.

In 1898 they offered rebore service in .25/21, .25/25, .32/20, .32 Long CF, .32/40 B & M, .32 Ideal, .38 Long CF, .38/55 B & M, or .38/40. Also out of the ordinary, Stevens rebored and chambered for the .40/70/330 Ballard 2⅜" cart-ridge. However, they did not offer this latter service for their own rifles but only those others "of suitable make." Stevens apparently never made any of their own rifles in a larger stan-dard caliber than the .38/55 Ballard and Marlin.

On the rebore barrels by Stevens which I have examined, the caliber was not restamped nor was there any indication that the rebore was by Stevens, however, "rebore" stamp-ings were made. The Winchester rebores or rechambers usually had an order number on the underside of the barrel under the forearm, but Stevens did not as far as I can ascertain.

By 1920 Stevens no longer offered the fancy single shot rifles. Their offering was limited to the following rifles in rim-fire calibers only: "Ideal" No. 44; No. 414 "Armory Model - The Most Accurate Rifle"; "Favorite" No. 17, 20 and 27;

"Marksman" No. 12; No. 26 "Crack Shot" and No. 14½ "Little Scout - A Real Rifle in Spite of the Price."

In 1938 the single shot falling block action rifles were limited to the No. 417 "Walnut Hill Target Rifle"; the No. 417½ (same as 417 except Sporting Model); No. 418, same as 417 differing in lever, forearm, and sights; No. 418½ was the sporting model.

The Ideal 44½ action was never revived or offered for sale after 1915. All center fire factory 44 actions were also dropped, although the "Walnut Hill" was chambered very briefly in .22 Hornet. The cartridge proved to be too potent for the 44 action, and it was quietly dropped. After World War II the No. 44 Stevens was completely dropped as a discontinued item. The last single shot rifle on the 44 action was shipped from the company in 1947.

Chapter 7

REMINGTON RIFLES 1870 to 1907

1874 Remington Rolling Block long range Creedmoor rifle made for the International Matches. Windgauge front sight, long range tang sight which could be moved to heel of stock for prone shooting using the reclining method.

In advertising the "Long Range Creedmoor Rifle" in the December, 1875 issue of *The Field,* the following statement was made by E. Remington & Sons, Chicago Office, 237 State St.

"The best breech loading rifle in the world, used by Major Henry Fulton, Colonel John Bodine, and L. L. Hepburn in the International Rifle Match at Creedmoor September 26, 1874; and Major Fulton, Colonel Bodine, General Dakin, A. V. Canfield, Jr., and R. C. Coleman at the Great International Match, at Dollymount, Ireland, June 29, 1875, making the highest score ever known; also, used by the same gentlemen in all the matches following in Ireland and England, winning all the first prizes, including the Spencer and Association Cups by Coleman, who in the match for the Spencer Cup made 47 out of a possible 50 at 1000 yards, and in the same match at Wimbledon, on the 19th inst. for the Association Cup made 49 out of a possible 50 at 1000 yards. On the same day Fulton won the St. Leger Stakes making 35 out of a possible 35."

The fine rolling block Remington was based on the Sporting Rifle No. 1 first produced in 1866. The caliber was the same as the government issue and was a .50/70 caliber. Later, after the Henry rifle was produced by Winchester, Remington produced a buffalo gun based on the .44/90/400 which was also used by Sharps.

In 1872 one of the orders was for a .50 Sporting Rifle from Fort Abraham Lincoln in Dakota Territory by G. A. Custer, Brevet Major General U.S. Army. In a letter dated October 5, 1873, General Custer tells of his use of this rifle on the Yellowstone Expedition in glowing terms.

In 1873, when the Irish Rifle Team challenged the Americans, there were no target rifles which could be used to compete, yet the Amateur Rifle Club accepted the challenge and turned to Remington and Sharps for help. Both companies agreed to make the rifles free and put up $500 to help make up the United States' side of the stake.

The Remington Company turned to one of its own men who was a well known marksman, and this was L. L. Hepburn. Hepburn was the foreman of the Mechanical Department. Through careful designing and good workmanship the Remington Creedmoor became known as the most accurate long range rifle made.

In examining a Creedmoor Remington, if you take off the forend you will find the final approval of inspection in the stamped name L. Hepburn on the underside of the barrel.

The Creedmoor rifle uses a bottle neck .44/90/550 cartridge. The bullets, of course, were paper patched. The groove diameter is .452.

The Creedmoor Rifles were delivered in March, 1874, and the Amateur Rifle Club members began their practice. The full story of the match will be found elsewhere in this book. The Creedmoor Rifle was manufactured from 1873 to 1890. It was chambered for the .44/90/550 B.N., the .44/100/500 B.N., and the .44/105/500 B.N. The very early Creedmoors had 32 inch octagon barrels; later models had half octagon, half round barrels. The front sight was a vernier windgauge, and the rear a vernier sight giving elevation. The stock was a pistol grip, crescent rifle plate on the early ones and a shotgun plate on the later ones. A special sight plate was mounted at the rear on the comb of the stock, and when shooting long distance the sight stem was removed from its base on the tang and placed in the plate on the stock. The rifle was fired from a reclining position with the muzzle resting on the crossed feet and the left arm behind the head holding the butt. The sight, therefore, on the butt stock was necessary to get it close to the eye.

The Remington Rolling Block No. 1 was produced in many military models as well as in three sporting types.

The Remington Mid Range was manufactured from 1875 to 1890 in calibers from .40 to .50-70 GOVT. The barrels were 28 or 30 inches long and were half octagon and half round. Stocks were both straight or pistol grip types. Pistol grip stocks and forends were checkered, forend tip was horn. Sights to buyers' wishes.

The Remington Short Range model had half octagon barrels 26 inches long and was chambered in .38 extra long to .46 rim and center fire. The stocks could either be straight or pistol gripped, and there was a choice of sighting arrangements. This model was manufactured from 1875 to 1890.

The Remington Black Hills Rifle, according to the 1877 Reduced Price List, was offered in .45/60 center fire. The barrel was 28 inches long and round. The stock was straight. This was manufactured from 1877 to 1882. Normal chambering was .45/70 GOVT.

In the 1877 list the No. 1 and No. 2, as well as the Long Range Creedmoor, are all shown with octagon barrels. This is also true in the 1882 catalog.

The No. 2 Sporting Rifle was chambered in .22 and .32 rim fire and in center fire in .32, .38, .44, .25/20, and other .25 calibers as well as .44/40, .38/40, .32/20. The barrel was octagon in the length of the buyer's choice with a straight grip stock and curved butt plate. Sights were a matter of choice. The early models were marked E. Remington Sons, Ilion, N. Y. Later models bore Remington Arms Co., Ilion, N. Y., U.S.A. Both markings appear on the top flat of the octagon. This model was manufactured from 1873 to 1910. The No. 2 action is much smaller than the No. 1.

Remington Buffalo Rifle Model with No. 1 action was made in round or octagon 30 inch barrel and was chambered for calibers such as .40-50 Sharps, .44-90-400, .50-70 GOVT., and .45/70 GOVT. This rifle was made from 1872 to 1890. The barrel markings were the same as the No. 2 Sporting Rifle. The patent dates appear on the left side forward part of the action.

One model which the catalogs list and which I have never seen or else not recognized is a Remington Deer Rifle in rolling block type in .46 long rim fire. The barrel was 24 inch octagon; the stock was straight.

Another graceful looking rifle of the Remington line is the No. 3 Improved Creedmoor in a Hepburn falling block side lever action. Barrels were 34 inches long in either octagon or round. Chambered for the .38, .40, .45 and others. Target sights, pistol grip stock, checkered, as was the forend. Some had cheek piece stocks and set triggers. Manufactured from 1880 to 1907.

The Remington No. 3 in the High Power Model was chambered for the cartridge of the buyer's choice all the way up to the Sharps .45-105. All No. 3's had set triggers on special order. Barrels full octagon, 26 inches, 28 inches, and 30 inches.

The match Rifle No. 3 was a mid-range version of the No. 3 Improved Creedmoor. Barrels were 28 to 30 inches in half octagon. The butt plate was Schuetzen horned style and nickeled.

The No. 3 was also made in a Long Range Military Creedmoor with full length forearm and apparently only in .44/75/520 caliber. The butt was shotgun shape with pistol grip, and both stock and forearm were checkered.

Another No. 3 was the Hunters Rifle, 1883 to 1907, and is quite rare. It had an underlever modification designed by L. N. Walker of the Remington Company. The Walker Rifles used half octagon barrels in 26, 28, and 30 inches and were chambered for a variety of calibers. Sights were a matter of choice, but open sights were standard.

Like all rifles manufactured at that time, variations in sights, stocks, barrels could be ordered to suit the individual, so many rifles are found which simply do not fit the description for that particular model. The collector, then, is faced with many problems whereas the shooter is concerned mainly with the rifle's capabilities to produce good groups or scores.

While there are many other target model rifles which were produced by Remington, the main concern of this book is with the popular single shot rifles of the 1870 to 1907 period.

Chapter 8

BALLARD RIFLES

40/70 Marlin Ballard, Winchester 5A telescope, double set triggers, Schoyen pattern butt stock, Schuetzen prong butt plate, Scroll engraved, case hardened receiver.

The Ballard rifle was originally the idea of C. H. Ballard who was a machinist. Under date of November 5, 1861, patent letters #33631 were issued to C. H. Ballard as an *Improvement in Breech Loading Fire Arms*. The application witnesses were Hartley Williams and R. Ball who were co-owners and operators of Ball & Williams Manufacturing Company of Worcester, Massachusetts.

In 1862 Ball & Williams were located on School Street in Worcester and employed one hundred men in the manufacture of the Ballard rifle. Mr. Ballard at this time was a foreman, and in 1865 he moved up to the position of superintendent.

These early rifles had a sliding extractor in the forend, manually operated and are curiosities and desirable collection pieces. These early rifles and carbines were made both as civilian guns and for the military. The sporting rifle of 1861 was made in .32, .38, and .44 long rimfire. The military carbine was made in .54 and .56/56 Spencer rimfire.

The military carbine of 1863 was made in .44 long rimfire. In 1864 the War Department purchased 1,500 of these.

Kentucky bought 3,000 of these carbines for its militia, and in 1864 ordered 15,000 additional Ballards in a rifle style in .46 long rimfire.

Of the first 3,000 contract pieces a number were made with a nipple device on the breech assembly to permit a soldier to use muzzle loading and a percussion cap if their supply of metallic cartridges was exhausted.

January 5, 1864, and antedated December 19, 1863, a patent was issued to Joseph Merwin and Edward P. Bray of New York as an improvement on the Ballard Rifle. The patent number was 41166. This patent is the one which enables the gun to be fired with metallic rimfire ammunition or as a muzzle loader with a percussion cap using a spent rimfire case.

Oddly enough, the original patent papers No. 33631 provide for an enclosed self extractor, yet when the gun was manufactured it had the manually operated extractor on the forearm.

In 1864 the business was taken over by the Merrimack Arms & Mfg. Co. of Newburyport, Massachusetts. This company continued to manufacture the Ballard rifle at Worcester until 1866 when it was transferred to Newburyport. The rifle was manufactured until 1869 when again the ownership was transferred, this time to the Brown Mfg. Co. On July 23, 1873 the Brown Mfg. Co. was ordered sold at public auction for failure to pay their indebtedness. At this time Daly of Schoverling & Daly of 84 Chambers St., New York, wholesale dealers in guns, bought the patent rights to the Ballard.

It was Mr. Daly who arranged with John M. Marlin to manufacture the Ballard again. Marlin was already established as a firearms manufacturer of pistols, but the Ballard was the first rifle to be manufactured. This production began in 1875 as a "Hunter's Rifle" in .44 rim or center fire.

From 1875 to 1881 the rifles bear the following marking on the left side of the frame: "J. M. Marlin, New Haven, Conn. U.S.A. Ballard's Patent Nov. 5, 1861"; in 1881 the marking was changed to "Marlin Firearms Co., New Haven, Ct. Patented February 9, 1875 Ballard's Patent Nov. 5, 1861." Also the marking "Marlin Firearms Co. New Havent, Ct., U.S.A. Ballard's Patent Nov. 5, 1861" is found. The markings are interchanged without regard to numbers in the case of the latter two markings. The marking regarding the February 9, 1875 patent is found only on rifles which had the reversible firing pin making the rifle either a center fire or rim fire.

Low numbered receivers were forged from a poor grade of steel and they have raw unconsolidated carbon throughout the forging, and below the five thousand number strain flaws can be found. Better forgings were used in the later models although both frames are entirely adequate and safe if not cracked through. However, do not try to anneal the receiver on the low numbers or you will end up with a ruined receiver. Somewhere around sixteen thousand number Marlin began using a cast receiver, and both forged and cast receivers will be found for all numbers above sixteen thousand. The receivers are both adequate in strength and were used on all caliber guns. Inspection of the inside of the receiver is the only clue as to which you have. Core marks are found in the cast receiver. Both types of receivers were casehardened in colors.

The main concern of our discussion is the period from 1875 to 1892 during which time the receivers bore the Marlin name. The first rifle by Marlin was a Hunter's Rifle in .44 long rim and center fire. The firing pin was reversible.

In *Forest and Stream,* January 20, 1876, there was an announcement that the Ballard rifle would be manufactured by J. M. Marlin using his improvements. The advertisement was sponsored by Schoverling & Daly, wholesale dealers in firearms of New York City. In the April 27, 1876 issue there was an advertisement that Schoverling & Daly could make deliveries of the new Ballard in various models. Throughout the life of the Ballard rifle Schoverling & Daly continued to advertise the advantages of the rifle. The various models are listed below.

Hunter's Rifle No. 1 - round barrel 26, 28, 30 inches long. .44 long rim or center fire.

Hunter's Rifle No. 1½ - 30 and 32 inch round barrel, forged frame, Rocky Mountain open sights. .45/70 and .40/65. $22.50 to $24.40.

Far West Rifle No. 1¾ - same as No. 1½ but with double set triggers. $26.00 to $28.00.

Sporting Rifle No. 2 - .32, .38 long rim or center fire, .44 Long CF, .44/40 Winchester, .32/20 Winchester. Round barrel 26, 28, and 30 inches long. In 1881 this was offered in octagon barrel 24 to 30 inches long, reversible firing pin, plain stock, forend and sights. $15.00.

Gallery Rifle No. 3 - .22 short and .22 long rim fire. The .22 long rifle had not yet been developed by Stevens. Octagon barrel in 26 inch length, pistol grip stock. "Offhand" Swiss pattern nickeled butt plate, plain walnut forend. The lever loop is long like the Winchester's.

Target Rifle No. 3½ - 30 inch octagon barrel, peep and globe sights, shotgun butt stock, checkered. Forend checkered. Everlasting .40-65. Price $35.00.

Perfection Rifle No. 4 - .40/70 Sharps, .44/77 Sharps bottle neck, .50/70, .38/50 Everlasting, .40/65 Everlasting, .44/75 Everlasting. Also made in other large calibers according to buyers' wishes. These rifles were used for both hunting and target work so the sighting equipment included vernier sights as well as telescope mountings if the shooter paid the extra price. In 1881 this rifle was offered in 30 inch octagon barrel, Rocky Mountain sights, and wrought frame. The calibers were .32/40, .38/55, and .40/63. (The .40/63 is the same as the .40/70; however, in changing over from folded head cases to solid head cases the case only held 63 grains of black power, so the "new designation") .

Mid Range Rifle No. 4½ - 30 inch half octagon barrel, butt stock and rifle same as No. 7. Caliber .40/65. Price $45.00.

Mid Range Rifle No. 4½ Al - same as No. 4½ except had engraved frame. Everlasting .38/50 and .40/65 calibers.

Price $58.00. Spirit level and windgauge front sights added, $60.00.

Pacific Rifle No. 5 - Big bore calibers .45/70 GOVT., .40/70 Sharps, .40/85 Ballard, .40/90 Sharps, .44/77. Sharps B.N., .50/70 GOVT., .38/50, .40/65, .40/90, .44/75, .44/100, of the Everlasting cases. Also in .38/55, 40/63, and .44/40 Winchester. Heavy octagon barrel 30 to 32 inches long, double set triggers, forged frame, ramrod under barrel in thimbles, Rocky Mountain sights. Recommended for buffalo, elk, deer, and bear. The favorite of the plains and mountain hunters. $22.00 and $24.00.

Schuetzen Rifle No. 6 - 32 inch barrel, half octagon, double set triggers, vernier receiver sight, windgauge front, straight grip stock, cheek piece, checkered, Swiss butt plate nickeled. Checkered forend, horn tip. Engraved frame scroll pattern with bear on left side and deer usually on right. .32/40 and .38/55. Price $57.50.

Off Hand Rifle No. 6½ - Rigby 28 and 30 inch long round barrel. Vernier receiver sight, windgauge front, pistol grip, cheek piece, checkered stock, Swiss butt plate nickeled. Forend checkered with horn tip. Scroll engraved frame. Single trigger, long loop lever. .32/40 and .38/55. $57.50. Also furnished with shotgun style butt stock and rubber flat heel plate if desired. (I have seen this latter plate made of horn.)

Long Range Rifle No. 7 - 34 inch half octagon barrel. Long range vernier receiver sight, windgauge front sight. Sights had a morocco leather case furnished for them. Shotgun type butt stock, pistol grip, checkered rubber or horn plate. Forend was checkered with horn tip. Single trigger, long loop lever. Engraving was from $5.00 to $50.00 extra. If engraved, had "Ballard A1" engraved on side of receiver. Without engraving $65.00 in .44/100 Everlasting.

Long Range Rifle No. 7 A1 - everything the same as No. 7 but the barrel which was Rigby and the engraving was standard. The price was $80.00.

Union Hill Rifle No. 8 - this was the target rifle that was so well liked. 28 and 30 inch half octagon barrel, pistol grip stock, cheek piece, checkered, "Off-hand" nickeled Swiss butt plate, double set triggers, graduated receiver sight, globe front. Calibers .32/40 and .38/55. Stock and forend were checkered. The lever loop was the long type like Winchester.

Union Hill Rifle No. 9 - same as No. 8 but with single trigger. $30.00.

Schuetzen "Junior" Rifle No. 10 - same as No. 8 but with 32 inch barrel. $42.50.

The Ballard enjoyed a high degree of popularity from 1875 through the 1880's. By 1890 the demand for the rifles had dropped, and the financial recession or depression of 1893 probably decided the company to drop the rifle entirely. By 1890 the catalog still listed Model Nos. 2 and 3. The 1891 catalog listed no Ballard rifles among the Marlin Arms listings. C. H. Ballard, like Christian Sharps, faded into obscurity although the fame of his invention continued.

In 1868 Mr. Ballard severed his connection with the manufacture of the Ballard Rifle, and in 1869 he moved to 9 Mt. Vernon Street, corner of Winsor. Mr. Ballard died August 9, 1901 at the age of 79. The *Worcester Telegram* and the *Worcester Gazette* carried this obituary notice August 10, 1901:

"H. Charles Ballard - Death of inventor of rifle bearing his name in Civil War Days.

H. Charles Ballard, inventor of the famous Ballard rifle, died late last night at his home, 9 Mt. Vernon St., aged 79 years. He had been healthy until early this week, when he was prostrated. The cause of death was dysentery.

Mr. Ballard, previous to the outbreak of the Civil War was foreman in the factory of Ball and Williams on School street and in 1860 obtained patents on a breech loading rifle which later was used extensively. In 1862 Ball & Williams employed 100 men in the manufacture of the rifle which was of 42 caliber and especially adapted to cavalry use.

Some years ago Mr. Ballard retired from business, although he maintained his interest in machinery and especially in fire arms. He was a member of Worcester lodge IOOF in which he has held highest office. His wife survives."

WARNING. If you examine a Ballard rifle and cock the hammer before you open the action you will break the web on the hammer. Many Ballard hammers bear the result of some novice who didn't know better. I have watched modern shooters do this when examining a Ballard without thinking. They do not do it to other makes nearly as much. The reason is puzzling.

Note: The No. 5½ Ballard was the same as the No. 5 except it was chambered for the Sharp's .45 2⅞″ cartridge and had a 30″ barrel.

The No. 6 was also made in .38/50 with a Farrow butt plate.

BALLARD.

The New 40-70 BALLARD CARTRIDGE fits all 40-63 Rifles.

The Ballard Rifle is superior to all others for gallery purposes. It is more accurate, safer, and easier to manipulate, and it comes up to the shoulder better than any other.
J. M. CONLIN, White Elephant Gallery, New York.

I have a Ballard .22 caliber that has fired nearly one million cartridges and NEVER COST A CENT FOR REPAIRS. I will shoot the Ballard against any other make of rifles.
CHARLES D. TAYLOR, Shooting Gallery, 18 Beach St., Boston.

Representing Nos. 2, 3 & 4.

No. 2, octagon barrel, reversible firing pin, using rim and center fire cartridges, 32 long and 38 long, and .44 Colt and Winchester Center fire. .38 caliber are made 30 in., 8¼ lbs. .44 caliber are made 30 in., 9 lbs...........$22 00
.32 caliber are made 28 in., 8½ lbs.

No. 3, GALLERY RIFLE, octagon barrel, .22 cal.—24 inch, 7¼ and 8¼ lbs................$21.00   26 inch, 8 lbs................$25.00.
No. 4, octagon barrel, wrought frame, Rocky Mountain sights, using everlasting shells, 38-50 and 40-63—40-63, 30 inch, 10 lbs........$25.00.   38-50, 30-inch, 9½ lbs................$25.00.

Myself and partner are using Ballard Pacific Rifles, 40 caliber, and I would not exchange mine for any other rifle I ever saw. The breech action and shells are simply perfect.
T. K. GURNEE, Kit Carson, Col.

No. 5, PACIFIC RIFLE, octagon barrel, double set triggers, cleaning rod under the barrel, with extension rod and brush, Rocky Mountain sights, using everlasting shells, also .44 W. C. F. and .45 Government cartridges, 30 inch, $30; 32 inch, $32.   45-100 ever-
40-63 everlasting are made 30 in., 10 lbs. .44 W. C. F., 11¼ lbs.   40-90 everlasting 30 in., 10½ lbs., 32 inch, 11½ lbs.   45 Government, 30 in., 10 lbs., 32 in., 11 lbs.   lasting, 30 in., 11 lbs. 31 in., 12½ lbs.   44 W. C. F., 30 in., 10 lbs.
No. 5½, MONTANA RIFLE, same style and finish as No. 5, weighing fourteen lbs., shot gun butt, .45 cal., 2% in., Sharp's cartridge, 32 in. barrels, $32.

The Ballard Off-Hand and Schuetzen are without question the most accurate and best balanced rifles I have ever handled.
W. MILTON FARROW, champion Off-Hand Shot of the World.

No. 6½, P. G. OFF-HAND RIFLE, Rigby barrel, mid-range Vernier peep and wind gauge sights, fine English walnut stock, modified Swiss pattern, pistol grip, upper row butt plate, exactly fitting the arm, finely engraved, and every part highly finished, using everlasting shells, 38-50, 28 and 30 inch...................$70 00

No. 7, A 1 LONG RANGE RIFLE, Rigby barrel, finely engraved, extra handsome English walnut stock, rubber butt plate, every part made with the greatest care, and finished in the highest possible style, using the new thin and everlasting shells, .45 cal., 100 grains.

No. 6, SCHUETZEN RIFLE, octagon or half octagon barrel, double set triggers, Marlin's short Vernier mid-range peep and wind-gauge sights, Swiss pattern, hand-made, polished selected stock, nickel plated butt plate, full octagon, finest finish, using everlasting shells, 38-50, 30 in., 13 lbs., 32 in., 15 lbs.

No. 4½, A 1 MID-RANGE RIFLE, half-octagon barrel, fine English walnut stock, Marlin's improved Vernier peep sight, graduated to 800 yards, wind gauge front sight, bead and aperture disks, finely engraved frame, rubber butt plate, every part finished in the best manner, using everlasting shells, 40-65, 30 inch..........$65 00

No. 4½, LONG RANGE RIFLE, half-octagon barrel, 34 inch, Marlin's improved Vernier peep sight, graduated to 1,300 yards, wind gauge sight with spirit level, bead and aperture disks, morocco sight cases, hand-made pistol grip stock, full checquered regulation weight and pull, using everlasting shells, 44-100...................$75 00

SCHOVERLING, DALY & GALES, Agents, 84 and 86 Chambers Street, New York.

SEND FOR FULL DESCRIPTION.

19-11-10m

Original Ballard advertisement which appeared in the November 10, 1883 American Field.

Chapter 9

THE MAYNARD RIFLE

In 1885 the Maynard Rifle Catalog noted that "ten years ago almost everyone was calling for rifles to shoot 1,000 and 1,200 yards, with charges of powder and lead enough to shake the constitution of a mule. Many riflemen found themselves suffering from the effects of it and soon began to look for sport behind a much lighter charge of powder and lead. This led to a more general adoption of the .38 and .40 calibers with from 40 to 70 grains of powder. Now we find that the great part of the target practice is at 200 yards' range and the great call is for a still smaller caliber and lighter charge."

The Massachusetts Arms Company, who made the Maynard, offered their Model 1882 in .22/10/45, .32/35/165, and .35/40/240 center fire cartridges. By 1885 they suggested that if the shooter wished to use .32 or .38 rim fire ammunition, then they should select the Model 1873.

The Model 1882, besides being offered in the above calibers, was also offered in .50/70 .50/100,, .55/100, .44/60, .44/70, .44/100/520, .44/100/550, .40/40, .40/60, .40/70, .38/50, .35/40, and .22 rim fire.

The Model 1882 was vaunted for its simplicity, compactness, accuracy, safety, and durability. The parts in a Maynard were all made of steel, including the receiver and no malleable iron was used in its manufacture. The barrels were especially and finely made. The workmanship was of the best.

I have found in shooting the heavy calibers in a Maynard rifle that the shooter takes quite a bit of recoil punishment unless one has a Mid-Range target rifle in either Model 1873 or 1882. A. E. Leopold, one of the famous shots of the early days, used a Maynard No. 1 Creedmoor with a 32 inch barrel. After Leopold's death A .O. Niedner bought the rifle from the family and kept it for many years. It was a .44/100. One Maynard I had used a .44/100 in a short barrel, and although the barrel was heavy the recoil was too much. In .32 or .35 or .22 the Maynards are pleasant little guns to shoot and very accurate.

There were three basic models of the Sporting Maynard Rifle. The original Sporting Maynard was the Model 1865 which used a cap on a nipple and a brass case inserted in the breech. All Maynards, including the original Civil War .50 caliber, have the same action and many parts are interchangeable with the exception of the barrels. The barrels were made to fit a particular model and will not interchange with other models. Incidentally, don't go too much on this interchangeability in models either; if you are strictly a collector it will not make any difference, but if you are a shooter check the headspace on those barrels and when found to be all right, keep that barrel with that action. If you don't know how to check headspace, better have some competent gunsmith do it before shooting it - in fact, that goes for any of the old single shot rifles. Do not take an old unknown rifle, cram a shell in it, and hold it up to your face to shoot; in fact, do not hold it at all! Tie the gun down to a heavy timber or across an old automobile tire; put the butt inside the tire and lash the barrel firmly, then run a string from the trigger and stand a long way back and touch it off. If it is still in one piece, examine the case for any sign of irregularity. If there is any, do not shoot the rifle until the problem is corrected. Then refire the rifle four or five times with the rifle tied down. It takes more time; it is more trouble; but the old newspapers carried accounts of someone in the old days who was just as foolish only they usually did not live.

The Model 1873 used a very thick headed cartridge case which was Berdan primed. The Model 1882 used shells which were either Berdan primed or Winchester primed according to the buyer's wishes.

The two target rifles which are especially fine are the Model 1882 No. 15 and No. 16. The only difference being the No. 15 forearm was not checkered and differed in pattern from the No. 16; the wood in the butt stock was plain and had no pistol grip. The No. 16 had a pistol grip checkered stock and forend, both of fancy wood. Both models used vernier sights rear and windgauge front.

Another desirable but rare rifle is the Maynard Creedmoor Rifle of 1873 known at No. 14. The caliber was .44/100, weight just under 10 pounds, single trigger as were all Creedmoor rifles, vernier sights, windgauge front. Price was $70 in 1880. The pistol grip on this rifle was attached to the loop in the lever. The stock was a straight grip with shotgun butt. There was no forearm. The barrel was a No. 4.

There were many testimonials to the fine shooting qualities of the Maynard in almost all the sporting publications of the day. July, 1885 *The Rifle* carried the following note.

"At the Spring Meeting of the Lawrence (Mass.) Rifle Club, May 30, 1885, Mr. E. F. Richardson, with a Maynard Rifle, made 27 consecutive bull's eyes, at a distance of 200 yards, off-hand, on a paper target. The score is the best on record to date.

On May 9, 1885, Mr. W. H. Taft, of Brattleboro', Vt., made in a regular match, with a Maynard Rifle, at 200 yards' distance, off-hand, 117 out of a possible 120, on the Massachusetts Paper Target, a score which has never been excelled."

Another excerpt was from the *Forest and Stream*, July 23, 1885 as follows:

"At the grounds of the Lawrence Rifle Club, this afternoon, the best record for off-hand marksmanship at 200 yards in the world was beaten by Mr. E. F. Richardson, who used a Maynard .35 calibre rifle, with which thirty-one consecutive bull's eyes were scored, beating the best previous score, that of H. G. Bixby of Nashua, N. H., at Walnut Hill in 1882."

The Massachusetts Arms Company recommended a bullet temper of 1½ to 2 per cent tin to pure soft lead as working the best. The bullet lubricant recommended was one part beeswax to three parts of beef tallow. They also offered the following advice in using paper patched bullets in their rifles:

"Wipe the mouth of the shell *perfectly clean* to prevent *crimping* or *tearing* the patch. Prime the shell. Then with a charger fill it so that the butt of the bullet will lightly press the powder after it has been jarred down by tapping the shell. Enter the bullet into the shell by hand, and use the loader to *true it up* and *press it home*. Use water to clean the barrel, (avoid using oil while shooting,) and see that it is *cleaned perfectly* after each shot. If lubricator is used, use but a trifle, and as evenly as possible. An atom of beef's tallow wiped around the patch with the thumb and finger after the bullet is placed in the shell and just before shooting, works well. We think it improves the shooting of the patch bullet to *slit the patch* (with the point of a sharp knife after it is placed in the shell) from the shell toward the point on the opposite side of the lap in the paper."

The 1882 Maynard has a very unique safety device built into the action, and if you have one of these it might be well to check to see if it is free and operating. In the milled space directly below the firing pin hole is a tapered bar protruding from a milled recess in the receiver. The thin pointed end should be toward the hammer. There is a small coil spring recessed into the bar which makes the bar work. The bar is pivoted on a small screw on the right hand side of the receiver, forward. The flat part which sticks out of the milled recess should be downward and the rounded part on top. As the action is closed, if this bar is working, the hammer moves back away from the firing pin, relieving the tension on the pin as the cartridge is seated home.

If in reassembly you do not position this bar correctly, when the action is closed it will be locked. Do not force the action, but disassemble the rifle by taking out the forward pivot screw as well as the sliding locking bar. Correct the position of the safety bar and then reassemble.

A group of Southern Ute warriors. The picture was taken in the late 1870's. Note the 1873 Maynard the well-armed warrior in front of the door is holding.

Chapter 10

SHARPS RIFLES

A. O. Zischang .32/40 Sharps 1878 with windgauge front sight, false muzzle, bullet starter, double set triggers, mid-range rear vernier, cheek piece pistol grip stock, and prong type butt plate.

It is hard to imagine someone who calls a Zischang Sharps Borchardt, with a false muzzle, starter, and beautiful Swiss butt stock and plate "a messed up gun." That such a purist exists I can vouch for. Probably no one in the world knows as much about Sharps rifles as this person, yet he is strictly interested in the factory produced rifle. This person is none other than Mr. Frank Sellers of Denver, Colorado. Mr. Sellers' collection of Sharps Rifle Company materials is well known. He has owned the original records as well as existing equipment of the company. So it was he who set my thinking straight, and who has supplied the information from primary sources in regard to the Sharps rifles that we are here interested in.

Frank also graciously supplied me with photographs which are illustrated herein from guns that have been in his collection.

In the first place the term "1874 Model" that everyone refers to is a misnomer. The Sharps Manufacturing Company changed completely on January 5, 1874 to The Sharps Rifle Company. All officers of the company changed, and in all probability the "Model 1874" designation was used by the new company to denote this complete change. This term was used for the first time in the Sharps Rifle Company catalog of 1878.

I personally had never questioned the "Model of 1874" designation until I read the official account of the Indian attack on "Adobe Walls", Indian Territory, June 27, 1874. During this engagement twenty-eight men and one woman were engaged in an attack by hundreds of mounted Indian warriors who were not in the mood to exchange niceties. Eight or nine of the men and the woman were residents of the settlement; the rest were buffalo hunters, and this the Indians had not counted on. Billy Dixon, a buffalo runner, made good use of a Sharps "big 50" that had just been delivered to James

Hanrahan the saloon owner, and there was no doubt Dixon knew how to make good use of the new rifle.

The Indians were driven off with a small number of casualties among the defenders, and within a few days the settlement was filled with more buffalo hunters congregating for safety. These men depended upon their rifles and knew them, and the Indians were not about to renew an immediate attack in the face of such opposition.

The first sporting rifle *made* for a metallic cartridge was a side hammer Sharps Sporting Rifle which left the factory June 20, 1869 and was known as the 1869 Model. The caliber of the rifle was .44/60 bottle neck Sharps cartridge; the rifle had a 26" octagonal barrel, double set triggers, globe sights, pewter tip on the forearm, weight about 10½ pounds, and was made in Hartford, Connecticut. The rifle was shipped to a John Wilson of Providence, Rhode Island.

In December, 1870 the first of the guns later to be known as the Sharps Model 1874 was shipped from the factory.

The only difference between the 1869 and the 1874 Sharps side hammer rifles was in the thickness of the lock plate. The 1869 Model has the thicker plate. There were 60 sporting rifles of the 1869 Model shipped before the complete change-over to the 1874 Model. In both the 1869 and 1874 Models all new parts were made and used in all sporting rifles made by the Sharps Rifle Company. None of the Civil War carbine or rifle parts were used in the production of Model 1874 arms.

All brass cartridge sporting Sharps firearms which have octagonal barrels and no markings on the barrel are rifles which have had the barrels replaced, and somewhere on the barrel will be found a crown or other foreign proof mark. These barrels were purchased under contract by various sporting goods dealers and were made in both England and Germany. Some of the barrels were rifled with the Sharps rifling; some were of the English type rifling; and some were German. A well known Civil War surplus dealer of New York still sold these barrels in the 1930's. The barrels were formed to Sharps outside contours, dimensions, and threading. They were manufactured as replacement barrels. The one I have is English, but has the normal Sharps rifling. It is identified by no barrel markings except a crown underneath the forearm.

Oddly enough along with the regular manufacturing process Sharps did contract rebuilding of Civil War Sharps carbines and actions. Private companies in the sporting goods line would buy up thousands of these actions, then have Sharps rebuild them. Schuyler, Hartley, and Graham Sporting Goods Dealers of New York, had Sharps convert six or seven thousand of these actions, and these were the rifles which were sold at such reduced prices. This practice began in 1876 and the reasoning is indeed strange, for they were causing their own competition! The markings on the barrels were standard Sharps markings, including "Old Reliable." The military carbines and rifles used the original barrels and just "Old Reliable" was added to existing markings. Sharps Rifle Company 1879 catalog mentions the conversion for individuals desiring the change as follows: "Sharps Rifles made prior to 1864, and adapted to use linen or paper cartridges, cannot be transformed into metallic cartridge arms except at such a high cost as to render it impracticable."

In 1880 when the solvent Sharps Rifle Company decided to quit their business, E. C. Meacham of St. Louis bought at auction the machinery and parts of the company.

E. C. Meacham advertised in the sporting goods journals of the 1870's and 1880's as the E. C. Meacham Arms Company Armory, St. Louis, Mo., U.S.A. In the July 28, 1883 *American Field* they advertised as follows:

"Sharps Sporting Rifle Model '78 round barrel 26 inch, 8¼ lbs., .40 caliber straight shell, 70 grains. $20.00

Sharps Sporting Rifle Model '78 octagon barrel 30 inch, 11 lbs., .45 caliber 2 1/10 shell, 70 or 75 grains. $22.50

Sharps Sporting Rifle Model '78 octagon barrel 30 inch, 10 lbs., .40 caliber, 65 grains. $21.00

The .45 cal. can be rechambered to take the 105 grain shell if desired at an extra expense of $1.00.

Sharps New Military Rifle .45-70 caliber, length of barrel 32 inches, length of rifle 48½ inches, weight without bayonet, 9 pounds. $15.00"

At this point it might be well to mention that the largest number of military model rifles, both in the side hammer and the 1878 Borchardt model, were not made for or sold to the U. S. Army. These rifles which are known as the military models were purchased principally by civilians and state militia groups.

The E. C. Meacham Company used the machinery and stampings of the Sharps Rifle Company and converted around two thousand Civil War Sharps actions to sporting rifles known as 1874's and to military models. The only way to tell these rifles from the originally produced Sharps rifles is by the markings. The stamps on the barrels have thicker letters and are deeper than regular Sharps Rifle Company markings.

From 1869 to 1877, which takes in the period of the side hammer models, the .44/77 bottle neck Sharps cartridge was the most popular chambering. The .50/70 Government cartridge was the second choice in chamberings requested.

The Borchardt action model which became known as the 1878 Model was first shipped from the factory in November, 1877!

The beautiful accurate rifles in the "1874" Model made for the International matches were known as the "Creedmoor" model. However, the company never referred to these rifles after January, 1876 as being "Creedmoor", rather they and the "1878" Model were called "Sharps Long Range Rifles."

In the "1878" Model the .45/70 Government cartridge was the most requested chambering, with the .45 - 2⅞ inch Sharps being the second most requested. If the Borchardt rifle was chambered in other than .45 caliber, it is most unusual.

The 1875 Model advertised in the 1876 catalog never reached actual production. Only two of these rifles are known; one is a beautifully made complete rifle that looks like a very high grade target arm and is known as a Sharps Long Range #1 Model. The other is an action only. The 1875 was the Borchardt patent with an outside hammer. The rifle which went into production as the Model 1878 was a hammerless improvement on the Model 1875.

Sharps did make some factory produced Schuetzen rifles. There were 69 of the Model 1874's made. When the New York Central Schuetzen Corps sent in an order for 66 of a rifle designed for their use, the Sharps Rifle Company engaged the service of Charles E. Overbaugh, a company shooter, who designed and caused to be manufactured the proto-type as shown in the accompanying picture.

Prototype 1874 Sharps Schuetzen developed by Overbaugh of the Sharps Rifle Company for production. In production this was slightly modified.

The only change made in the production of the arm was to eliminate the short brass forearm and substitute the usual wood checkered forend. Of the 69 1874's made, about half had palm rests and "German" cheek pieces. This rifle was made from July, 1877 to October, 1878. Only one of these barrels is known to have been round; the rest were octagon shape and thirty inches long.

In the 1878 Model, 153 Schuetzen rifles were made using the same general pattern of 1874.

The palm rest of the 1874 Sharps is rather distinctive and looks like an old fashioned door knob. The shank of the palm rest which engaged the forearm was nonadjustable and simply slipped into a german silver inlay with a hole in the forend. Since there was no way of retaining the rest in the forearm, most of them were readily lost; and since there weren't many to begin with they are very rare.

All long range rifles were tested by Frank Hyde, a well known company shooter and an accurate marksman. In 1878 Hyde won the Wimbledon Cup at the Creedmoor Range, firing a Sharps Long Range Rifle with a score of 143 out of 150 at 1,000 yards. For the grand aggregate prize in the same match, F. Hyde, Col. H. F. Clark, and Capt. W. H. Jackson, all using Sharps rifles, tied on a score of 300 points.

For these long range rifles Sharps made a loading tube for the powder so that the rifle could be loaded from the muzzle. By using this tube no powder ever was left in the bore. The tube was of brass slightly less than bore diameter and was 37 inches long with a funnel on one end. The tube was offered in 1878, 1879, and 1880.

Sharps molds are quite distinctive and were made by Sharps. Having read both criticism and half praise of the Sharps molds, I borrowed one and tried to cast bullets in it. Believe me! If I were a buffalo hunter I, too, would have bought my bullets already patched as most of them did! It's nice to have one of the molds to show with a gun, but don't think you are going to use one with satisfaction.

After Sharps sold out in 1880, the Bridgeport Gun Implement Company who made loading tools bought Sharps stock and manufacturing tools, so Sharps molds marked BGI Co. were made after this date. Incidentally, I did see a mold made on the Sharps pattern by B. G. I. Co. marked on the right handle M.F.A.CO. and on the left handle Cal 45-420. The B.G.I. Co. stamp was not on the mold. Interpreting the above, it was a Bridgeport Gun Implement Company, Sharps pattern mold made for the Marlin Firearms Company in .45 caliber, 420 grains weight, and was for the Ballard rifle.

Following is a compilation of material which Frank Sellers has researched and which is published here for the first time concerning information on the loading equipment furnished by the Sharps Rifle Company.

SHARPS LOADING TOOLS, PRICES

	1874-75	1876	1877	1878	1879	1880
Mould, Sporting	3.00	3.00	3.00*	3.00*	2.50*	2.50***
Mould, Express	-	-	-	-	3.50**	3.50**
Mould, Long Range	4.00	4.00 ⎱	10.00*** ⎱	10.00*** ⎱	8.00*** ⎱	8.00***
Swage	4.00	10.00 ⎰	⎰	⎰	* ⎰	6.00*
Wad Cutter	.75	.75*	.75*	.75*	.50**	.50**
Cap Awl	.25	.25*	.25*	.25*	-	-
Lubricator Mould	.50	.50*	.50*	.50*	.50*	.50*
Follower	.50	.50*	.50*	.50*	.50*	.50*
Charger	.25	.25	.25*	.25*	.25*	.25**
Bullet Seater	1.00	1.00*	1.00*	1.00*	.75**	.75**
Brass Loading Tube	-	-	-	3.00***	2.50***	2.50***
Shell Crimper	-	-	-	3.00***	-	-
Shell Reducing Die & Punch	-	3.00	6.00	6.00	4.00***	4.00***
Re-Decapper	-	-	-	-	1.25**	1.25**
Base & Nose Trimmer	-	-	-	-	-	-
Complete Set, Sporting	-	6.00	6.25	6.25	5.00	5.00
Complete Set, Express	-	-	-	-	6.00	6.00
Complete Set, Long Range	-	-	12.25	18.25	15.00	15.00

*   Included in Sporting Set   **   Included in Express Set   ***   Included in Long Range Set

When the Sharps Rifle Company changed over to the 1878 Model they had this comment to make in regard to their use of round barrels: "It is an established fact, proven by years of experiment, that a round rifle barrel is stronger, and will give better results, where extreme accuracy is required, than an octagon or half octagon. The metal is equally distributed around the bore, thereby ensuring equal expansion. In an octagon shape it is much more difficult to obtain the even distribution of the material. The octagon shape originated before machinery for turning barrels was in use, and gun makers found it an easier form to make than the round, by hand filing. In the interest of fine shooting, it is to be hoped that the octagon will go out of fashion at an early date."

Their hope was not to be realized, for the love of the octagon barrel shape is still with us today. Stevens, Ballard, Remington, and others could not completely abandon the design demanded by gun enthusiasts; however, they did compromise by making the so-called half round-half octagon barrels. This term, however, is a misnomer for actually the barrels are about 1/3 octagon and 2/3 round. Today Winchester has revived the octagon barrels on their commemorative rifles and find that the octagon barrel still appeals to many.

In 1879 the following note appears in the catalog:

"The history of Sharps Rifle is generally well known, but it may be briefly stated that it was invented in 1848, and was the first successful breech loader ever made. A company for its manufacture was organized at Hartford, Conn., in 1851, which carried on the business there for many years with very great success. In 1875, a new company was formed with its present title, under a special charter from the State of Connecticut, with an authorized capital of one million dollars. Early in 1876, the new organization erected an armory at Bridgeport, Conn. (a manufacturing centre, ninety minutes by rail from New York), where it has about 90,000 superficial feet of working room upon a site of twenty-two acres, on the line of the N.Y.N.H. & H. R.R. with navigable water on the premises, and with every facility in the way of machinery and tools for turning out the best of work.

Sharps Rifles of all descriptions are specially noted for the following qualities:

I. SAFETY. — Although hundreds of thousands have been in use during the past thirty years by soldiers, hunters, sportsmen, and others, yet no instance has occurred of injury through any defect of system, workmanship, or material.

II. ACCURACY. — See the records of all the great rifle

matches and the testimony of experts and celebrated shots, nearly all of whom use the Sharps arms.

III. DURABILITY. — Large numbers of the rifles made in 1852 and '3 are still in use, and apparently as good as ever. (It is worthy of note that at the close of the late "unpleasantness," SHARPS RIFLES AND CARBINES were the only arms of all the various breech-loaders purchased or made by the government that were retained and are now in use by the United States Army. All others, *without exception*, were sold, or condemned and broken up.) General Steele, who used SHARPS RIFLES on the Texas frontier for many years, reports that he never had occasion to send one to the gunsmith for repairs.

IV. The ease with which the several parts can be kept clean and in working order. — The barrel is open to instant and unobstructed inspection, and can be brushed or wiped from the breech, thus ejecting the debris from the muzzle — a decided advantage over those than can only be wiped from the muzzle, throwing the debris into the working parts.

Western and other hunters and marksman have, as their estimate of its excellent qualities, long given the name of "Old Reliable" to the Sharps rifle, and the company adopted that as their Trade Mark, which will appear upon all of its *productions*.

Sharps Rifles and buffalo are almost synomonous in American thinking, and while the following letters do not mention the Sharps Rifle they do point out, in a brief span of time, the havoc wrought by the hunters and the total disregard of wildlife preservation.

American Field, January 22, 1881:

Leadville, Col.

Editor: — Ten years ago hunting on the plains was attended with considerable danger as well as hardship. The Indians were quite numerous, and when favorable opportunity presented itself, decidedly hostile. Game in great variety was abundant, but the buffalo was generally selected by the hunter as his victim.

Two modes of warfare are adopted. One is for a party of horsemen to make a sudden dash upon a herd; kill and maim all they can, and run the balance out of the district. All the meat thus killed is invariably left upon the ground to rot. Sometimes a few tongues are saved. If a wounded bull turns upon his adversary the horse always carries his rider out of harm's way. This kind of hunting can be pursued without much danger. The other kind consists of hunting on foot. The wind, inequalities of the ground, high tufts of grass, or any substance affording temporary obstruction from view, are all taken advantage of. If still without range, crawling, snake-fashion, is resorted to. The moment one of the sentinels of a herd throws up his head to gaze at the approaching object, said object must remain perfectly motionless until the sentinel lowers his head, fully satisfied that no danger is imminent. Once within range, and a cow or calf successfully disposed of, a good hunter not unfrequently can kill from half a dozen to a score. I have known of an instance in which one hunter killed forty out of one herd, and that from the precise spot at which he commenced shooting. On one occasion myself and partner got within range of a small herd of sixteen bulls, cows and calves, and in half an hour had secured the last one of them. My first attempt to bring down a buffalo was a failure. After infinite pains in the way of creeping and crawling amongst the cactus (known on the plains as the prickly pear) I succeeded in placing myself within two hundred yards of a herd. Whilst regaining breath I chose for a target a splendid looking fellow who stood broadside to, evidently ignorant of my proximity. Taking careful aim, I fired, and distinctly heard the thud of the ball against his carcass; instead of falling, as expected, he and his comrades started off on a lively lope, apparently uninjured. As long as they remained in sight my intended victim held his own in the race, and finally disappeared. My next attempt was more successful. In going down a ravine and turning a sharp angle I brought up face to face with a bull buffalo. We stood and looked at each other a short time when my friend slowly wheeled about face and commenced retiring. In a moment he received the contents of my rifle and fell. As he did not appear to be wounded fatally I thought to hasten his demise by giving him another dose of lead. Out of six cartridges left every one in turn unaccountably missed fire. Being determined to secure him, the hunting knife was my only available weapon. Laying aside my rife, I cautiously crept up to him and drove the knife into his side. Quick as a flash he jumped up, and followed me up the steep bank. When almost on the top he weakened and returned to the bottom of the ravine. This attack and retreat business was repeated six or eight times before the bull was completely vanquished. In indulging in a foot race with an infuriated buffalo, no time nas as yet been recorded, but the pace is generally fast. It is much pleasanter to be a spectator than a participant. A cowardly pair of legs are more to be desired than a stout heart. A person who retains his presence of mind, can evade the charge of the animal by repeatedly doubling back. Buffalos are less given to fear, and consequently more easily approached, during the latter part of the afternoon than at any other time.

I have not been on the plains during the past nine years, but am informed that all kinds of game have almost entirely disappeared during the interval. Buffaloes for several years were killed just for their hides. One man, to my own knowledge, had saved up during a single Winter season 3,000 of them. The prices they brought ranged from $1.75 to $2.50 each; saddles of buffalo and antelope sold readily for $5; deer were worth $7, and the skins of beaver and otter $5 each. A hunter in those days could make big wages, but later, as they became more numerous, and the game less abundant, they with difficulty gained a precarious living. I presume by this time hunting buffalo as means of livelihood is almost one of the things of the past.

L. Cook.

American Field, October 27, 1883:

Mr. R. G. M. Graham, we learn from the Sioux City *Journal,* has returned home from a hunt in the Judith Basin, M. T.:

"He and a few of his English friends outfitted at Livingston about six weeks ago, and have since been enjoying wild life in what was supposed to be the buffalo country. But the buffalo have gone. What was the heart of their range up to within a year ago is now about as free of buffaloes as Iowa is. While on the hunt news came of a bunch of some 3,000 that had walked down from somewhere north of the Powder River. Mr. Graham and his party worked down that way, but long before they got there they learned that the herd, excepting a few bulls scattered in the mountains, had been killed off by half-breeds and white hunters. It is not believed there is a herd of buffaloes of any considerable size, if, in fact, there are any except scattered individuals, south of the British line. While the party was in the Judith Basin a cloud of smoke came that settled over the entire country, lasting for eight days, so that an object could not be seen more than two hundred yards away. They afterwards learned that this smoke came from prairie fires started by the Indians north of the Missouri to keep the buffaloes from going south, as is their habit at this season of the year. If this fire accomplishes its purpose it will keep the small remnant of the once myriads of the buffaloes north of the boundary line, where they are likely to die of cold and starvation, if not killed off by the hungry Assiniboine Indians.

"In brief," remarks the Sioux City *Journal,* "the noblest of

American game animals is all but extinct, and next season only scattering individuals are likely to be found anywhere on the continent."

Too true, too true; but is the *Journal* aware that the Government, if it does not openly encourage the destruction of the buffalo, winks at it, as the most effective means of controlling the Indians. The more numerous the buffaloes the more independent are the Indians, and consequently more difficult to control.

Then the white settlers on the frontier do not regard the buffalo as the noblest of American game animals, but as a nuisance they cannot be rid of too soon, as a herd of buffaloes not only brings a swarm of Indians, but when it stampedes it often carries off one or more herds of cattle.

With so many enemies to contend against, the buffalo must necessarily become extinct before the march of civilization."

As a sequel to these stories I might add my own comments and experience with the Sharps Rifle and the buffalo.

On December 9, 1969 at the Colorado Tamarack State Wildlife Area near Crook, Colorado and under the direction of Wildlife Officer Gardner of the Colorado Game, Fish and Parks Division, I was allowed a legal hunt for buffalo. The animal which was to be taken was a two and a half year old bull.

I approached the herd which indicated a watchful interest, but no alarm and managed to get within seventy-five or eighty yards of the group before it was decided that for safety sake I had better take my selection. This was not an enclosed herd but one out on the rolling prairie, and there was no place to hide or run to in the event the herd decided to break.

I used the cross sticks that the old hunters used, knelt, rested the long barrel across the sticks, and waited until the bull turned his head. Suddenly the moment came, and the big Sharps roared. The bull's knees buckled, and he dropped to the ground as the 437 grain flat point slug driven by 9 grains bulk shotgun powder and 90 grains of FFG black powder did its work.

There was no need for a second shot. The rifle used was an 1878 Sharps Borchardt long range rifle with a 34 inch round barrel with vernier windgauge front sight and vernier rear target sight. The bullet used was lubricated with Alox and beeswax and was cast from a Winchester .45 flat point mold. The rifle when fired with this load was capable of 2½ inch groups at 100 yards.

One of the most amazing things to me about this hunt was witnessing the "death dance" of the buffalo described by the old time buffalo hunters and the Indians. As the bull dropped, the herd all threw up their heads and noted that one of their number was down. Immediately the herd formed a ring around the fallen bull. While they all bellowed two buffalo tried to gore, or help — I couldn't decide which — the fallen one; then the first two stepped back into the ring and two or three more took their place. This strange "death dance" kept up for quite a while, then suddenly on signal the entire herd gave a "woof," heisted their tails in the air, and took off in a wild stampede in that peculiar rolling gait which keeps them going for miles.

In one brief moment of time I had joined the ranks of the old hunters, and I had done it with a Sharps!

Chapter 11

THE WINCHESTER SINGLE SHOT RIFLE

A NEW RIFLE!

WINCHESTER SINGLE SHOT.

WEIGHTS
FROM
7 TO 11½ LBS.

According to caliber
and size and length
of barrel.

Can now fur-
nish guns for
the following
sizes center-fire
Cartridges:

.32 ex long, .32,
.38 and .44 Win-
chester; 32-40, .38-55, .40-60 and .45-75
Winchester; 40-50 S. S., .40-70 S. S., .40-70 and
.40-90 Ballard; .40-90 S. S., .45-70 U. S. G., .45-
Sharps, .45-60 Winchester.

RIM-FIRE GUNS NOW READY.

WINCHESTER REPEATING ARMS COMPANY,
New Haven, Conn.

Send for 76-Page Illustrated Catalogue.

Winchester advertisement of February 18, 1886, American Field

[59]

The February 18, 1886 issue of the *American Field* carried an advertisement on the front page announcing "A NEW RIFLE" and the advertisement pictured a high wall in a thin wall model, single trigger, and chambered for the .32, .38, and .44 Winchester; .32-40, .38-55, .40-50 S.S.; .40-70 SS; .40-70 Ballard; and .45-70 USG. The weights were advertised as being 6¾ to 12 pounds according to caliber and size of the barrel. This advertisement also announced "Rim-fire Guns, Not Yet Ready."

The .22 rim fire known as the "Winder Musket" was presented to the public around 1905, although some list this as being brought out in 1907. The rifle was also chambered in .22 short during and after 1914. Gradually the .22 musket was accepted and the rifle attained a certain fame as a target shooting rifle. The National Rifle Association approved of its use in competition, and both the National Guard and the regular army made wide use of the rifle for military indoor target shooting and preliminary outdoor practice. The rifle was officially known as the Winchester .22 caliber musket. The gun was made in both "high wall" and "low wall" models. The Winder model was discontinued in 1920 when the first Model 52 target rifle was advertised.

Sometimes a modern rifle enthusiast will erroneously state that the Winchester single shot rifle was a "Buffalo Rifle." By the time the Winchester Model of 1879 was produced in 1885 the buffalo were long gone. This does not mean that these fine rifles could not bring down a buffalo, but rather that they were produced at a date when the buffalo herds had long been eliminated by the wanton slaughter of the 1870's.

In 1893 Winchester pictured three single shot rifles based on the high wall action. The "Special Sporting Rifle" had an octagon barrel, plain trigger, fancy walnut checkered pistol grip stock, and a rifle butt plate. This could also be obtained with a shotgun type butt stock. $30.00. The "Special Single Shot Rifle" had a half octagon barrel, fancy walnut checkered pistol grip stock with a Swiss butt plate, case hardened frame in colors, plain trigger, mid-range vernier rear sight, and a windgauge front sight. There was no slot cut in the barrel for a rear sight. $46.00. The "Plain Sporting Rifle" had a octagon barrel, plain trigger, plain walnut stock in either rifle or shotgun type, and a case hardened in color frame. The rifle butt stock had a plain butt plate. $15.00.

The fancy factory Schuetzen rifles did not appear in the catalogs until after 1900.

In the 1893 catalog the Winchester Company offers a

variety of calibers to suit the buyer's taste. These guns will be made for the following sizes of rim-fire cartridges:

.22 Short. .22 Long. .22 Extra Long. .22 Winchester. .32 Short. .32 Long. .25 Stevens.

The standard length of barrel of the .22 caliber rim-fire rifle will be 24 inches, and of the .25 Stevens and .32 caliber 26 inches; and these lengths in No. 1 barrel will be sent unless otherwise ordered. For the above cartridges no barrels will be made heavier than the No. 2.

They will also be made for the following sizes of center-fire cartridges:

22 W. C. F.	38 Express	40-60 W. C. F.	45-90 W. C. F.
25-20	40-70 Straight	40-65 W. C. F.	45-70
32 W. C. F.	40-70 Ballard	40-82 W. C. F.	45 Sharp's
32-40	40-90 Ballard	44 W. C. F.	45 Express
38 W. C. F.	40-90 Sharp's	45-60	50-95 Express
38-55	40 Express	45-75 W. C. F.	50-110 Express

Guns taking the .22, .32, .38, and .44 W. C. F. and .25-20 cartridges will only be made in the three smallest sizes of barrels, 1, 2, and 3. The standard length of the .22 W.C.F. will be 26 inches, and of the .32, .38, and .44 W. C. F. and .25-20, 28 inches. These lengths and the No. 1 barrel will be sent on all orders unless otherwise specified. For the other sizes of center-fire cartridges mentioned in above table, guns may be had with any size of barrel except the No. 1. The standard length will be 30 inches, and this length with No. 3 barrel will be sent on orders.

To accommodate all tastes as to weights of single shot rifles, five sizes of barrels will be made, numbering from 1 to 5, and varying in weight.

No. 1 barrel is the smallest, and will be adapted to the .22, .25, and .32 rim-fire cartridges, and to the .22, 32, .38, and .44 W.C.F. and .25-20 cartridges. Guns with this size of barrel will weigh from 7 to 8 lbs., varying according to caliber and length.

No. 2 barrel is intended for the same cartridge as the No. 1 when a heavier gun is desired, and guns with this size of barrel will weigh about $8\frac{1}{2}$ lbs., varying according to caliber and length. If very light guns are desired for the larger sizes of center-fire cartridges this barrel can be furnished for them.

No. 3 barrel is intended for large sizes of military and sporting center-fire cartridges, and guns with this size of barrel will weigh from $8\frac{1}{2}$ to 10 lbs., according to caliber and length.

A .32 caliber with 30 inch No. 3 barrel will weigh about 9¾ lbs.; a .38 caliber about 9½ lbs.; a .40 caliber about 9 lbs., and a .45 caliber about 8¾ lbs.

No. 4 barrel is made to accommodate those wanting a heavier gun, and will weigh from 10½ to 11 lbs. For this weight an additional charge of $2.00 will be made over the regular price.

No. 5 barrel is the heaviest which can be made, and will weigh about 12 lbs. For this weight an additional charge of $10.00 will be made over the regular price.

For extra lengths over those given above, $1.00 for every two inches.

.22 caliber barrels can only be made up to 28 inches in length. Other calibers can be furnished up to 36 inches only.

Set Triggers, additional _____ $2.00

Jointed Rod in butt stock _____ .50

When special barrel without slot for rear sight is wanted, an additional charge of $2.00 will be made, and no allowance for rear sight. The same charge will be made for changing the position of rear sight.

All .22 caliber single-shot rifles will be accompanied by a brass cleaning rod; other calibers, by a slotted hickory rod, without charge.

A short explanation about the action stresses the rifles' simplicity and strength.

This gun has the old Sharp's breech-block and lever, and is as safe and solid as that arm. The firing-pin is automatically withdrawn at the first opening movement of the gun, and held back until the gun is closed. The hammer is centrally hung, but drops down with the breech-block when the gun is opened, and is cocked by the closing movement. It can also be cocked by hand. This arrangement allows the barrel to be wiped and examined from the breech. In outline everything has been done to make the gun pleasing to the eye. It can be furnished with or without set trigger, with barrels of all ordinary lengths and weights, and for all standard cartridges; also with rifle and shot-gun butt, plain or fancy wood, or with pistol grip. All .22 caliber rim-fire rifles are fitted with a kicking extractor, which throws the shell clear of the gun.

TO DISMOUNT THE ARM

Take off the fore-arm. Take out the mainspring and ejector spring. Loosen the stop screw, and take out the finger lever pin. Draw out the breech-block by the finger lever with the hammer attached. The extractor will drop out. If it is desired to remove the trigger or sear, take off the stock. Remove the

side tang screws and tang; the pieces attached to the tang can
then be removed by pushing out the pins which hold them.
Remove the sear spring screw and spring.

TO ASSEMBLE THE GUN

Replace the sear spring and screw. Mount the trigger and
other parts of the lock on the tang, and slide it into place.
Replace the side tang screws. Assemble together the hammer,
breech-block, and finger-lever, and hold them in the same rela-
tion to each other as shown in the cut; that is, the firing-pin
protruding, and the hammer against the breech-block. In this
position push them from the under side of the gun partly into
position. Put in the extractor, and push the whole into place,
pull back the trigger, so that the sear may not catch on the
hammer. Put back the mainspring, ejector spring, and fore-arm.
Replace the stock.

The 1916 Winchester catalog which was the 50th anniver-
sary issue listed just five variations of the single shot falling
block action as standard offerings. The caliber listing included
all "desirable calibers from .22 to .50."

The "Sporting Rifle" was a high wall action, octagon
barrel, plain trigger, plain walnut stock and forend, and
had a blued frame. The price was $16.00.

The "Special Sporting Rifle" had an octagon barrel, plain
trigger, fancy walnut pistol grip rifle butt stock which was
checkered as well as the forearm. The price was $34.00. A shot-
gun butt stock and either a metal or rubber butt plate at the
same price.

".22 Caliber Musket" Standard and only style made.
Round 28 inch barrel, .22 short or .22 long rifle cartridge.
Musket, solid frame, $16.00. Musket take-down style $19.00.
N.R.A. sling $2.25. Designed Specially for Military Indoor
Target Shooting and Preliminary Outdoor Practice.

"Sporting Rifle Take-down," octagon barrel, plain rifle
stock and forend. Also offered with a shotgun butt stock,
$19.00. The low wall is pictured in this particular advertisement.

"Take Down Schuetzen Rifle," No. 3 octagon barrel, 30
inches long, no rear sight slot. Fancy walnut pistol grip stock,
new Schuetzen pattern cheek piece, new Schuetzen style butt
plate, stock and forearm checkered. Double set triggers, spur
finger lever, new style palm rest which was adjustable in
length and angle. Take Down, $62.00. Solid frame, $59.00.
Telescope A5, $29.00.

All the actions offered at this time were of the coil spring
type. The company still capitalized on the idea that the breech
block and lever were of the Sharps' pattern.

Also offered in the single shot rifle action style was a 20 gauge shotgun. The barrel was round, the wood was plain with the butt stock in shotgun pattern. Solid frame, $16.00. Take-down, $21.00.

In remarks about the Winchester rifling the company cautions the reader that "if the twist is too slow the flight of the bullet will be untrue and it will 'tumble' or 'keyhole' as it is called when a bullet passes through the air in a lengthwise position instead of point on. On the contrary if the twist is too quick or sharp the bullet is spun so rapidly that it is unsteady in its flight and wobbles like a top when it first begins to spin."

When shooting any of the old single shot rifles the shooter will encounter situations just as mentioned above. An examination of the target may indicate these conditions and if it does (obviously you cannot change the rifling), then experiment with the length of the bullet and the powder charge, within safe limits. Remember that most of the old rifles had pressure limits of 35,000 pounds in the best of them; many were made to operate around 25,000 pounds or less, so keep your loadings within safe limits!

The following numbers with the date of the manufacture may be of some value in trying to determine the approximate date of the manufacture of a particular Winchester single shot rifle:

YEAR	SERIAL NUMBER	YEAR	SERIAL NUMBER
1885	1 to 272	1893	59,801 to 65,798
1886	273 to 6,543	1894	65,799 to 69,086
1887	6,544 to 16,330	1895	69,087 to 73,771
1888	16,331 to 29,695	1896	73,772 to 76,197
1889	29,696 to 36,951	1897	76,198 to 78,872
1890	36,952 to 44,047	1898	78,873 to 82,256
1891	44,048 to 52,398	1899	82,257 to 85,086
1892	52,399 to 59,800	1900	85,087 to 87,544

Beginning with rifle number 87,545 manufactured in 1901 the single shot rifle numbers were inventoried and reported as of June 30. The following list is for rifles manufactured between January, 1901 and June 30, 1920. Serial number reported as manufactured as of:

YEAR	SERIAL NUMBER	YEAR	SERIAL NUMBER
June 30, 1901	89,800	June 30, 1911	113,000A
June 30, 1902	92,000	June 30, 1912	116,000A

June 30, 1903	94,000	June 30, 1913	119,000A
June 30, 1904	96,000	June 30, 1914	122,000A
June 30, 1905	100,700	June 30, 1915	124,000A
June 30, 1906	102,700	June 30, 1916	127,000A
June 30, 1907	105,000	June 30, 1917	130,000A
June 30, 1908	107,000A	June 30, 1918	133,000A
June 30, 1909	109,000A	June 30, 1919	136,000A
June 30, 1910	110,000A	June 30, 1920	139,500A

Although the rifle manufacture was officially discontinued as of June 30, 1920, rifles were assembled and sold subsequent to this date.

The high wall thin side receivers are found in all serial numbers as are the thick side receivers; however, there were not as many thick side receivers sold.

The original high side receiver at the front of the receiver was octagonal in shape. The one I have is a .32/40 octagonal barrel, thin side receiver, single trigger, and bears the number 972. The name of the company is on the barrel in block letters, but the caliber and the serial number are in a "script" type form. This form of receiver was changed around 7,000 serial number with the top form of the receiver having a radius or rounded form.

The serial number on this single shot rifle is found on the lower tang, and the tangs were easily changed. Replacement tangs were not numbered and on many reblued rifles, when the tang is polished for the rebluing process, the lightly stamped serial numbers are removed. In the days not too far in the past this was unimportant.

Low wall receivers seem to have made their appearance in the 5,000 series of the serial numbers or around the second year of the manufacture of the rifle, 1886.

Two sizes of barrel shanks were used: .825 and .940. I have found .825 barrel shanks on two high wall receivers, but generally the .825 was on the low wall and .940 on the high wall. The thread is the American V, 16 threads to the inch.

The markings on the upper tang do not appear until after serial number 100,000. The A after the serial number indicates that this is a coil spring action. No flat spring rifles were manu- after 1907.

Receivers were case hardened in those made prior to June, 1902; after that date the receivers, like the rest of the rifle, were blued. For those who demanded it and ordered it, special case hardened receivers were available after this date. Some receivers were also nickle plated on special order.

The finest of the Winchester single shot Schuetzens were not offered until after the 1890's. Like Stevens, the rifles were short lived and by 1914 the demand for these rifles was fast diminishing. The early Schuetzen rifles had straight grip stocks, and it was not until 1898 that pistol grip stocks made their appearance.

Chapter 12

SOME GUNSMITHS OF COLORADO

Riflesmiths who made an impression on the men who used the rifles were likely to be remembered long after their deaths, and to many shooters the names of Carlos Gove, John P. Lower, George Schoyen, and Axel Peterson would be recorded on the list.

Carlos Gove was born in Wentworth, New Hampshire in the year 1817. He apprenticed to a gunsmith at Boston, Massachusetts when he was 16 years of age. In 1837 he enlisted in the United States Dragoons and after serving in the Seminole War was discharged in 1840 at Fort Leavenworth. He served as a gunsmith in the Indian Department and then after four years he opened his own shop in St. Joseph, Missouri. Later he moved to Council Bluffs, Iowa and acquired a farm. In 1860 he moved his equipment by wagon train to Colorado, and in 1871 he is listed as being at 12 Blake Street, Denver.

In 1873 Gove took in two more gunsmiths who were to become well known. One was John P. Lower and the other George Schoyen. Gove was a good shot, and the shop became well known. Gove rifles are highly prized by those who still have them. Gove died in 1900 at the age of eighty-three.

John P. Lower was born January 23, 1833 at Philadelphia, Pennsylvania, and at 18 went to work at the Grubb arms and ammunition store until 1858 when he became a salesman for the company. Lower worked for the company for 21 years. In 1868 he traveled over the new railroad line which the Union Pacific had built as far as Larimer City, Wyoming Territory. He returned to Cheyenne and then to Denver by stagecoach. After working for Gove he established his own store on Blake Street in Denver, and by 1876 he was well known and a friend to many including the Indians, particularly the Utes. John P. Lower died in 1917 at the age of eighty-four.

Not all the rifles which were stamped with the name "J. P. Lower — Denver" were altered or made by the Lower shop. Many of these guns bore the name simply to show that it was handled and sold by this well known company. Lower, like Gove was a rifleman and one can find his name listed at many of the old matches run by the Colorado Rifle Club.

George Schoyen was a native of Norway and came to the United States after the Civil War. He migrated to Denver from Chicago and entered the employment of Carlos Gove. Schoyen remained in the employment of Gove until 1885 when

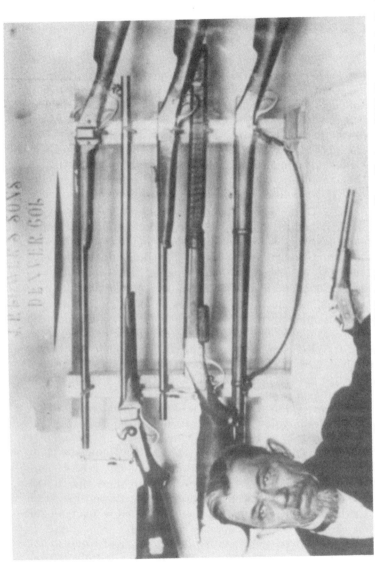

John P. Lower of Denver, Colorado. Picture taken about 1910 in his gun store. Top rifle is an 1874 Sharps. 2nd rifle is a fine Sharps 1874 Creedmoor presented to Mr. Lower. Third rifle is a sporter, type 1878 Sharps. Fourth rifle is a side panel 1878 Sharps long range rifle with gold lettering. (Note the added on barrel weight) Bottom rifle is a standard 1878 .45/70/500 military Sharps and is the one he used to fire the target of 1882.

George C. Schoyen Denver, Colorado. Picture taken before 1903.

Gove retired from active business. Schoyen and a man named D. W. Butt set up a partnership which apparently didn't last long. In 1887 he entered a partnership with F. A. Burgen. This latter partnership was quite successful and lasted 8 to 10 years. For a period of about 7 years he was in business by himself, then in 1904 Axel W. Peterson became his partner in the business at 1417 Lawrence Street, Denver. Mr. Schoyen, besides being a careful and fine workman, was a gentleman of the old school who went to work properly attired in a white shirt and tie and managed to always look the part of the gentleman regardless of the job.

In comparing barrels C. W. Rowland wrote to a friend in 1905 stating that as far as he could ascertain there was no difference in the barrels made by Pope or Schoyen. This is certainly a tribute to both men.

A. W. Peterson carried over the business from Schoyen and continued at the same address, later moving to 1429 Larimer Street, Denver. Schoyen died in 1916, but Peterson continued the business together with his son Roy until his death in 1946. Axel Peterson came to the United States from Sweden, worked in Chicago, and he too migrated westward to Denver in 1879 joining Schoyen in his work in 1904. Peterson was a true riflesmith in that he could and did perform work in all phases of the gun work. He is best known, however, for his fine barrels. Peterson also relined many guns, particularly in .22 caliber, and although for some strange reason modern collectors or shooters shudder at the word, these barrels shot as the finest.

Peterson is believed to have made around seven hundred barrels by his own count. He was also an excellent shot and many of the old matches record his name as a competitor. His favorite hunting rifle was a .45/70 Sharps Borchardt, but his best target scores were made with the .38/55.

Axel W. Peterson with a fine Ballard double set trigger rifle and a Malcolm scope.

Chapter 13

FRANK AND GEORGE FREUND

One of the finer gunsmiths of the West has often been glossed over, probably due to the fact that his work was concentrated on improving an already existing action. That man was Frank Freund, and closely working with him was his brother, George Freund.

Frank Freund was born in Heidelburg, Germany in 1837. He was a gun apprentice when in 1857 he emigrated to the United States and went to work for E. Remington & Sons. He continued to work for Remington until the Civil War when he enlisted in the Union Army. After his discharge he established a gunsmith shop at Nebraska City, Nebraska. After the Union Pacific built the railroad the town was bypassed, and the Freund brothers began moving west with the rails.

George was also born in Germany about 1840 and came to the United States in 1866, joining Frank as a gunsmith.

As the brothers moved west they established "branches" in ten different rail cities, moving along with the construction gangs. After the rails were joined and there was no need for the large gangs of men used in the construction, the Freund brothers as well as other "business men" had to find a place to settle where they could be assured of an income.

By 1870 they had found their way to Cheyenne, Wyoming Territory and then to Denver. They opened a shop at 21 Blake Street, moving to 31 Blake Street in 1872. In 1873 Frank helped form the Denver Deutscher Scheutzenverein, and during the same year he won a medal for the best made Colorado gun.

By 1875 the country was in a financial crisis, and the Freund brothers had to sell out to J. P. Lower and move back to their branch store in Cheyenne. While in Denver, the Sharps Rifle Company records show that Freund Brothers purchased 39 1874 Sharps Rifles.

During the next 3 years at Cheyenne, Frank received 3 patents on improvements to the Sharps 1874 model. The Sharps rifles have no camming action, and reloaders often found they couldn't get the shell into chamber except by forcing it in with whatever they had at hand. As part of his attempt to sell Sharps on the idea of his rocking or camming breech block Freund did a fair amount of research and found a surprising number of buffalo hunters who had lost an eye, fingers, etc., when the cartridge exploded as they were trying to force it into the chamber. I have encountered the same problem, and Frank Sellers says to mark the shell with a V nick on the rim and to always insert the case with this mark up and in the center. It doesn't completely do away with the problem, but it helps.

Unfortunately, Freund also found a goodly number of men who had been killed by the Indians during attacks when they, too, couldn't force the cartridge into the chamber.

In any case, Freund's patents and improved guns cured the problem. He was a prolific letter writer, and Sharps finally in disgust refused to consider his improvements. He even wrote to other people encouraging them to write in to Sharps endorsing and pointing out the need for his improvement.

Freund converted about 300 of the Sharps rifles to his improvement, and the rifles were of very good quality. They are marked F. W. Freund Patents, Wyoming Armouries, Cheyenne, W. T.

Sharps Rifle Company refused to send the Freunds rifles unless they were prepaid, and like dealers of those times they sold many more guns than they made. As was the custom of the day, they stamped their name, either Freund Bros. or Freund & Bro., on the barrels of the rifles sold. The one I have is an 1874 Military Model in .45/70 GOVT. with Freund & Bro. stamped on top of the barrel just behind the sight and longways of the barrel.

Most improved Sharps under Freund's patent were made after 1877 and in Wyoming. Some later ones were made in Jersey City, New Jersey, and some have been found with a Brooklyn, New York address.

Catalogs were issued by the Freund Brothers for the improved Sharps action and by Frank Freund for his improved rifle sight. Both catalogs are very rare.

During the time the brothers were in business in Cheyenne, Frank would get the wanderlust and go off, leaving George to tend the shop. In 1876 he was in the Black Hills of the Dakota Territory; later he made a name for himself in central Wyoming as a buffalo hunter. In December, 1876 he was in New York City and married Clotilda Gasperini. His wife didn't appreciate the wide open spaces when they returned to Cheyenne in January, 1877.

By September, 1878 the Wyoming Armoury was in finnancial trouble, and in 1880 Frank bought out whatever interest George had. George went to Durango, Colorado and in 1882 opened a gun store there selling sights; doing repair work; etc. He was the armourer for Fort Lewis, U. S. Army. On

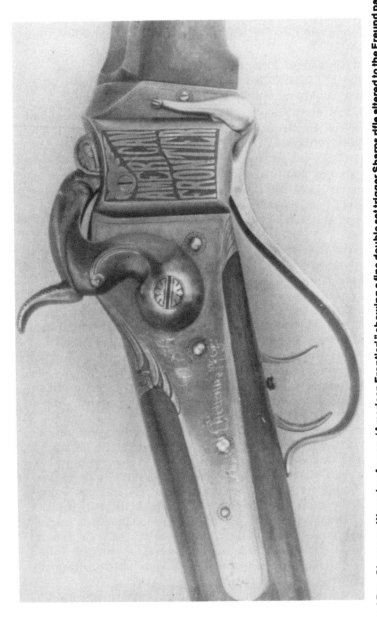

"Freund Bro. Cheyenne Wyoming Armory 'American Frontier'" showing a fine double set trigger Sharps rifle altered to the Freund patent. Collection of Charles Grimes, Littleton, Colorado.

June 21, 1891 a disastrous fire wiped out his entire business. George died March 25, 1911.

In 1885 or 1886 Frank closed the Wyoming Armoury and moved to Jersey City, New Jersey. In 1895 he broke his leg while working at the Brooklyn Navy Yards, and he never went back; instead he had a room in his home where he did gun work.

In 1905 he went to California and worked four years as a gunsmith. He couldn't make enough to move his family, so he went back east and again worked out of his home until his death July 27, 1910 at the age of 73.

Another Freund patent, #211728, dated January 28, 1879 was to make a hammerless action out of the Ballard and a device providing for automatic cocking of the set triggers.

One of the few assets Frank had was a patent #168834 for pistol grip attachments. Springfield Armoury used the patent and made the pistol grip attachments for the government military rifles in the 1870's and 1880's without payment. Mrs. Freund took this to court, but it was not until 1929 that the government finally settled the justified claim.

Chapter 14

GEORGE SCHALCK

George Schalck was born November 22, 1825 in Wiesbaden, Germany, and died October 21, 1893 at Pottsville, Pennsylvania. He learned the trade of gunsmith in his native Germany and emigrated to the United States in 1854 and set up a business at Pottsville, Pennsylvania.

The rifles which he offered for sale were made with barrels which were rifled with eight lands and grooves, the lands being more narrow than the grooves. The grooves, or rifling, were .007 to .008 of an inch deep, and the caliber of the barrel was usually from .32 to .45. The twist of the rifling was a gain twist with the rifling nearer the muzzle being at a quicker rate than that at the breech.

Schalck also used the false muzzle idea to protect the end of the barrel while the bullet was being loaded.

These improvements, the type and rate of twist of the rifling and the false muzzle were to make an impression on a young man by the name of H. M. Pope who would further develop and refine these ideas to reach a state of perfection in rifle shooting that was undreamed of.

Schalck also pioneered the idea of using a bullet with progressive bands being a little larger from point to base and using a lubricant in the grooves between the bearing bands. This bullet, after the molds were introduced by Pope, became known as the Pope bullet, but actually the original development was that of Schalck's. This bullet development did much to cause the "Chase" or paper patched bullet to become obsolete.

Schalck became a well known rifle shot, and although much of his work was confined to muzzle loaders he was willing to change.

Schalck did not invent the false muzzle nor did he invent the gain twist, but in using these ideas he did make a superior rifle barrel.

The first breech loading false muzzle rifle made in the world was one made by George Schalck on a Ballard Rifle for a man by the name of William Hayes, a well known shooter in the 1880's. Using all the skill he had acquired from making muzzle loading barrels, Schalck was able to make a new type rifle that was superior to the old, and H. M. Pope was to continue that tradition.

Chapter 15

HARRY M. POPE

This book is not intended to be a biography of any one person, but rather to furnish a so-called "thumb nail" sketch of those who were closely associated with the Schuetzen rifles and their shooting. The name Harry M. Pope is known to every serious shooter, but as time goes on, the name becomes a legend and legends have a way of becoming altered; and so for a more complete story of Harry M. Pope I would suggest the book, *The Story of Pope's Barrels* by Ray M. Smith.

Harry M. Pope was born August 15, 1861 in Walpole, New Hampshire and died October 11, 1950 in Jersey City, New Jersey.

Pope began his working career for his uncle who had a bicycle factory. In 1881 he attended Massachusetts Institute of Technology. Later he manufactured, in association with his uncle, the Pope-Hartford automobile.

In the meantime Harry joined a rifle club at Hartford and began shooting with them. His first serious rifle was a .32/40 Ballard. About 1887 he decided he wanted a .25 caliber barrel and because of financial reasons decided to make his own. Pope made both the barrel and cases, and this was later to be known as the .25/21/86 when manufactured by the Stevens Arms Company. Later he made a .28 caliber barrel which became known as the .28/30/120.

In 1888 he became acquainted with the Schalck method of rifling as well as the use of the false muzzle and the use of a brass cartridge case for loading. This unusual rifle was made by Schalck for Will Hayes upon Hayes' special order. The rifle proved to be especially accurate and was in a .33 caliber.

The rifle and the shooting qualities impressed Pope, and so he turned his attention to making rifle barrels after the Schalck pattern.

Pope is probably the one who developed the method of using a duplex load of smokeless primer and the rest black powder. He also developed a duplex powder measure to handle this type of loading.

In 1894 Pope began making barrels commercially. During this time he continued his own shooting interest and made some outstanding scores from the offhand position.

In 1901 the Stevens Arms Company bought him out, and he went to work for them, making the Stevens-Pope rifles. Stevens Rifles marked Stevens-Pope from number 1 to 1,250 were made by Pope; beyond 1,250 they were made by the company mechanic based on Pope's method. On December 31, 1905 Pope left Stevens for San Francisco. On April 17, 1906 he opened his new shop for business. On April 18, 1906 the earthquake that shook California completely destroyed his shop and everything he owned.

After this loss Pope went to Los Angeles, but soon he was back in the East. At this time he worked for the John W. Sidle telescope shop. When Sidle quit his business, Pope was out of a job. In 1908 he finally re-established himself at a shop in Jersey City, New Jersey in the old Colgate building, 18 Morris Street. Here he had his business until his death.

The barrels Pope made were made with time consuming care, and despite some statements to the contrary, he did lap his barrels as have all the barrel makers. Barrels with the Pope name have had all the inherent accuracy built into them; their condition or lack of it can only reflect on the owner, for the maker devoted the finest of workmanship and time in building a barrel that he could put a stamp on.

This is the man; this is the legend; there have been imitations of his work, but none have equalled the care and the name he gave his product.

Pope barrels rifled by Pope were so marked with his name. Accessories, including molds, palm rests, re and de-cappers, and lubricating pumps, have been duplicated or manufactured to the original Pope specifications. While this is a tribute to the man, it confuses the picture for unknowingly the collector may have a Pope pattern accessory but not necessarily one made by Pope. Many of the Pope items were made by Stevens after Pope left the company.

Harry M. Pope at his lathe.

Chapter 16

A. O. ZISCHANG

August O. Zischang was born in Saxony, Germany in in 1846. He emigrated to the United States in 1876. His first employment was with the Sharps Rifle Company at Bridgeport, Connecticut.

Later Zischang went to Syracuse, New York where he was in business with Nichols and Lefever. In 1879 he opened his own gunsmithing shop and began the production of target barrels which were to become known for their accuracy. Perhaps as a result of his association with Sharps, many of his finest rifles were to be built upon the 1878 Model Sharps hammerless action.

Zischang became well known in shooting circles and counted as his friends many illustrious shooters and sportsmen of the times. The Zischang name was one that was highly regarded by the offhand shooters of the Schuetzenverein clubs.

Dr. Hudson of the Denver Rifle Club was one of the top shooters of the nation who shot a Zischang .38 caliber barrel on a Remington Schuetzen action. The barrel was throated for breech seated bullets. His loading was 18 grains of Sharpshooter powder and 10 grains of Cream of Wheat on top of the powder. The Cream of Wheat (a breakfast cereal) was used to prevent the hot explosion of the powder from melting or deforming the base of the bullet upon discharge. This method of shooting proved very effective for Dr. Hudson. This loading was frequently used by A. O. Niedner during his Schuetzen shooting days and also by others. Experimentation in using such a load might prove successful in your own rifle.

Zischang recommended paper patched swaged bullets with parallel sides. The swaging operation on bullets to be paper patched always left a slightly hollow or concave base, and when the patch was rolled on to the bullet the end was twisted and neatly folded over and seated into the hollow base, making a very neat bullet.

Zischang's rifling was 6 groove with the lands being less than half the width of the grooves. Measurement of the land of one of his barrels indicates a land width of .058 inch and a groove width of .112 inch. A .32/40 barrel measures .315 inch groove diameter and a land diameter of .3215. The rifling twist is right hand and is one complete turn of the rifling in 14⅞ inches.

Zischang invented a mold to permit casting different length

bullets from the same mold; set triggers for the Sharps 1878 hammerless; as well as several other improvements.

Zischang continued active in his Syracuse, New York shop until his death May 21, 1925. The active management of the shop had, however, been turned over to William O. Zischang, his son, in 1919. William, who had joined his father in the business when he was 14, continued to operate the business until 1943 when he retired and the shop was sold, ending a long and colorful service to the American shooters.

Besides making fine barrels for the Sharps actions, Zischang also barrelled the standard actions of the times including many fine Ballards.

Abel Merchant, one of the old time shooters now gone, wrote me in 1954 that his fine Zischang .32/40 rifle which he bought in 1904 could be depended upon to hit a penny at 100 yards every time with a duplex load of 5 grains BULK of smokeless powder and 40 grains of FG Hazard black powder. Mr. Merchant told me he liked the Hazard powder because it left more moisture in the barrel than Dupont black powder and didn't cake the bore like the latter. Even so, he felt that only 10 or 15 shots could be fired before cleaning was necessary, so remember even with duplex loading it is necessary to clean the bore to get good shooting.

The gun shop where the fine barrels were made was known as the A. R. L. Zischang Company and operated at 541 N. Salina Street, Syracuse, New York. The business was opened by A. O. Zischang in 1879 and continued in business at the same address until in 1943 when William O. Zischang, the son, retired and sold the business.

The Zischang team, father and son, entered many of the old Schuetzen matches at Union Hill, New Jersey and Glendale, Long Island, New York.

William Zischang died October 29, 1956 after a long illness; he was 78 years of age at the time of his death.

.32-40 Zischang Sharps 1878 with 8 power Sidle Scope and Pope ring mounts.

.32-40 Zischang Sharps 1878 #103 Lyman rear sight and #17 front sight. Abel Merchant Nassau, N.Y. (deceased)

Chapter 17
ADOLPH O. NIEDNER

A. O. Niedner looking over a fine muzzleloading rifle he made for his own use. This rifle is described in Major Robert's excellent book on Muzzle-loading Rifles.

Niedner was born October 1, 1863 at Philadelphia, Pennsylvania. His father manufactured fire hoses, and Niedner was taken into the shop when he was thirteen as an ordinary workman.

When 18, Niedner left home. He bought a horse, camping outfit, and a Winchester and worked his way westward to San Francisco. From San Francisco he traveled south into Mexico. In 1880 he was in Arizona, and during the Apache uprising he enlisted in the cavalry and served until 1883. He had a streak of white hair across his scalp where an Indian bullet had creased him during one of the skirmishes.

After his discharge from the army Niedner went to Milwaukee, Wisconsin, where he joined the police force. Niedner was a member of the old Milwaukee Gun Club and repaired guns in his spare time. From 1885 to 1890 Niedner used a rifle John Meunier, the riflesmith and member of the club, made for him.

Meunier advised Niedner in his gun work and gave him much valuable information; however, when Niedner insisted that breech loaders were better than the muzzle loaders he lost Meunier's confidence.

About 1890-91 Niedner moved back to Malden, Massachusetts where the company his father owned was then located. Niedner felt that he couldn't work out his own life by working within the family business, so he opened a gunsmithing business of his own. His attendance and association at Walnut Hill Rifle Range added to his business, and his work was brought to the attention of Dr. Franklin W. Mann, author of the book, *The Bullet' Flight*. Niedner and Mann were friends until the latter's death in 1916. At the same time that Niedner was doing work for Mann, another gunsmith by the name of H. M. Pope was also. In fact, after the earthquake in San Francisco which destroyed everything he had, Pope wrote a letter to Niedner suggesting that the two form a partnership. Niedner discussed the proposal with Dr. Mann, and upon his advice declined the offer. Niedner and Pope were too much alike for a satisfactory partnership to have existed for any length of time.

During the period Niedner lived in Malden he became well known as an offhand shot, and his name will be found in the list of entrants in many of the matches fired at Walnut Hill as well as other ranges.

Niedner worked with many riflemen of the period and developed the .22 magnum based on the .32/40 case with a Mann base band bullet, the .257 Roberts, .25 Krag Niedner, .22

Phila. Mch 5/08

Mr. A. O. Niedner

Dear Niedner

Last June a July we corresponded a little with the idea of getting together in business but somehow or other the matter was dropped I have stubbed along some how since then working with hired machinery & tools not adapted to rifle work & could not get ahead enough with my small work to go in myself in my own line. Owing to change in ownership I had to get out Nov 1 & have been at odd jobs ever since, mostly south, & am just back here. What are you doing? would you still want to consider such an arrangement as we talked of then, I have my regular line of rifle work that I am sure can be renewed if I am only able beside this I have eight elevators & micrometers that I have worked

Three page letter written by H. M. Pope to A. O. Niedner March 5, 1908.

on all summer & for while there
is going to be a large demand. I
have too a new bullet mould, superior
to anything I have seen. A new
re & decapper somewhat like the one
I made at Stevens but cheaper &
better; An automatic mould for
casting bullets by machinery so
we could make & sell Pope bullets
or any other lead ones cheaper by
far than any factory product is
now sold & at a large profit at
that. I also have a design for
a cheap rifle & one for a Schuetzen
these of course would call for
capital to make in any quantity
but our business might lead up
to it. I've now quite a lot of special
tools, but no machinery & very little
cash. I've only barely kept above
water the last year, but there would
be no difficulty in case you go
with me in securing the mostly

etc to you so in case anything
should happen to ~~you~~ me, that you
would be protected, and if we got
a business started, my business &
shooting reputation would certainly not injure you.

I shall be glad to hear from
you, shall be at the address
below for a few days. I have
one or two offers that I am considering, but don't quite like to tie down
to people of no mechanical experience
while you & I, both expert workmen
& not afraid of work could make
things hustle.

        Yours sincerely,
          H. M. Pope
          603 No. 7th St.
          Philadelphia, Pa.

M. Pope
3 No. 7th
a. Pa.

PHILADELPHIA
MAR 5
7-PM
19 18
PA.

STATION
- S -

Mr. A. O. Neil

Niedner magnum, .22 Hinman, a necked down .405 Winchester, and .22 Niedner Magnum rimless which was a .22 on a .25 Remington case looking much like a modern .222, besides a number of others. Niedner told me also that he had made the chambering tools used by Charles Newton in making the Newton rifles.

In 1921 William A. Stolley, who was connected with the well known Heddon Bait Company, persuaded Niedner to move to Dowagiac, Michigan, the home of the Heddon Bait Company. Stolley agreed to put up the capital necessary to launch a good small gun manufacturing and repair business.

By 1922 A. O. Niedner was in business and turning out very fine rifles in bolt actions as well as single shot rifles. Niedner held very fond memories of Schuetzen days and lavished much more time than usual on a gun being made on the old Schuetzen pattern.

In the early years of the company a young man by the name of Thomas Shelhamer joined the group of workers and became one of the finest stock makers in the United States during the period the company was in business. Mr. Shelhamer left the company during World War II and opened his own shop. Mr. Shelhamer died in 1971.

Niedner's eyesight began failing, and he retired from the business in 1940. His wife, Josephine, died in that year and from that time until his death he lived at the old home, 524 Main Street, Dowagiac, Michigan. My own friendship with Niedner dated from this time until his death December 27, 1954.

Niedner served the community as elected mayor of Dowagiac and took an interest in local affairs during his active years. Nationally, he was one of the original supporters of the National Muzzle Loading Rifle Association, and always tried to attend each one of the Labor Day weekend national shoots; finally giving up the last years before his death.

Niedner's rifle barrels, which were hand made by Niedner himself when he was active in the company and in Malden, were as carefully made as the very finest. In ranking barrels, I would rank Zischang, Schoyen, Pope, Niedner, Peterson barrels in that order for workmanship and shooting qualities. But in any case, whatever the maker, if you are fortunate enough to own one of the barrels by any of these makers you know you have the finest.

Niedner had a varied life and one that remained interesting to him until shortly before his death at age 91, and I am pleased that I was included as one of his friends.

Niedner barrels made at Malden bear the name A. O.

Niedner, Malden, Mass. Barrels made at Dowagiac may bear the name Niedner Rifle Corp., Dowagiac, or A. O. Niedner, Dowagiac, Michigan. The latter marking appears on those rifles made by Niedner himself between 1922 and about 1928 when the business was expanded. Subsequent to this time the completed rifles bore the name of the Niedner Rifle Corporation.

My own Niedner is a J. M. Marlin Ballard, double set trigger, Niedner Schuetzen pattern cheek piece butt stock, a prong butt plate, a checkered forend with silver tip, heavy 30 inch round barrel, and target scope mounts. The caliber is .32/40. There is a Niedner type palm rest. Although the work is typical of the fine workmanship of Niedner himself, the barrel bears the name Niedner Rifle Corporation. Another rifle which I have bears the name A. O. Niedner, Dowagiac, Mich.

Chapter 18

W. MILTON FARROW

Milton Farrow was a very controversial person and generated much discussion whether he was shooting or just making his usual pragmatic statements regarding anything connected with shooting.

In 1876 Farrow bought a Ballard Long Range Rifle and commenced practicing at 200 and 500 yards with the firm belief that he could outshoot the U. S. Rifle Team members who had fired in the 1876 International Match.

On October 4, 1876 he entered a match at the Blackstone Rifle Range near Providence, Rhode Island, and won the match with a score of 86 out of 105 points. The ranges at which he fired were 800, 900, and 1,000 yards. His competition included some well known shooters of the day, including F. J. Rabbeth.

In the summer of 1877 he won the National Rifle Association first prize at the Creedmoor Range in New York with a score of 203 out of 225. Again the range was 800, 900, and 1,000 yards.

In June, 1878 Mr. Farrow won the King's Medal in the Sharpshooters' Union Schuetzenfest at Union Hill, New Jersey. In the autumn of 1878 he won the National Rifle Association match at Creedmoor and the title of "Champion Rifleman of the United States."

Mr. Farrow went overseas in 1878 and 1880 and won matches in England, France, Germany, and Ireland. In England he won the Wimbledon Cup and 100 pounds sterling.

In 1877 he went to New York City as an employee of the agents for the Ballard rifle to learn the rifle business. In his shooting Farrow used a .38/55 Ballard for his offhand work and a .40 or .45 caliber Ballard for the long range work.

On October 14, 1884 he was issued a patent for a new type of rifle, and on October 25, 1887 a second patent for improvements on this rifle was issued. The rifle was first made in a small personal shop at Holyoke, Massachusetts and later at Morgantown, West Virginia where he resided for several years. Later he moved to Washington, D. C. where he continued to live for fifteen years and also continued to manufacture the Farrow Rifle.

The Farrow Arms Company catalog which I have was originally issued at Holyoke, Mass., with a later overprint of Morgantown, W. Va., and must have been printed late in 1888 or early in 1889. In this catalog he lists a Farrow rear wind-

[89]

gauge sight, a bullet seater, a re and de-capper, and a triple mould in addition to or as accessories for the Farrow Offhand Target Rifle.

I have never found any of the Farrow made accessories. I have, however, owned one of the rifles. The caliber .40/70 was stamped on the muzzle end of the barrel; the barrel was made by the Providence, Rhode Island Tool Company and was typical of the Peabody- Martini barrels in contour and rifling. The action parts were not especially well finished, and tool marks were in abundance. The hammer was low set, and if your hands were cold it could easily slip when releasing the hammer from full cock. Although the rifle handled well as an offhand rifle, it was, in my opinion, overated and a good Ballard a much more desirable arm. The action was a sliding block type and certainly of adequate strength.

The rifle I owned bore the number 18; how many were made is unknown, but the rifle is rather scarce although three of the rifles appeared in a recent gun show.

The following is quoted from the catalog:

"This mechanism is the result of years of study and experiment. It is the sixth action invented by Mr. Farrow, and is the best. It has fewer parts and combines a greater number of advantages than any other single loading rifle yet manufactured. The vertically sliding breechblock presents a direct resistance to the line of fire; when in the act of closing it will force in a cartridge that protrudes one-eighth to one-fourth of an inch. The spring extractor is very strong and in one piece. The action is either self cocking or not, at the will of the shooter and when not full cocking the hammer remains on the safety notch. The barrel is easily detachable, without tools, and when put together it is positive and firm and will not work loose when shooting. The Rifle is made in all standard calibres, but the .32 is recommended for target shooting. Each barrel, rifled with our gain twist and shot according to directions, is guaranteed to place 10 consecutive bullets in a 4-inch circle at 200 yards. (Can you buy an off-hand target rifle elsewhere with this guarantee?) The breech-block is easily taken out and replaced by removing the lever screw.

The form and model of the Farrow Rifle is superior. It pleasing lines and balance have that perfection of 'fit and hang so carefully developed in the finest 'Kentucky' and other first-class muzzle loading rifles.''

The catalog also notes that other makes of rifles can be altered to the takedown system for $3.00. The takedown system was very much in favor during the 1890's and early 1900's because of the problem of transportation and the need to make a rifle that was compact and easily transportable. Schoyen and Peterson in making a takedown rifle relied upon a taper pin which goes entirely through the action and locks the barrel securely in place. This pin was also utilized as an anchor pin for the use of lever bullet seaters developed especially for this type of action.

Although I have not recognized any of Farrow's conversions to the takedown system, it is possible that he utilized much the same method of pinning the barrel in place, for it takes but a tap with some hard object to release the pin and the barrel can be screwed out easily by hand.

W. Milton Farrow was born in Belfast, Maine on April 18, 1848 and died at West Palm Beach, Florida on July 15, 1934.

Mr. Farrow moved to West Palm Beach about 1919 from Washington, D. C. and opened a small shop where he continued to manufacture his rifle. In addition to the manufacture of the rifle he repaired rifles and made tool room models for those wishing a pilot type firearm.

About 1929 a cyclone wrecked his shop and most of his machinery was destroyed. This disaster ended the manufacture of the Farrow rifles.

Farrow rifle #18 has a Providence Tool Company .40/70 barrel.

Chapter 19

TELESCOPIC SIGHTS FOR SINGLE SHOT RIFLES

Prior to the American Civil War telescopes were being fitted to percussion rifles. During the war a number of heavy rifles were equipped with telescopic sights and used for sniping purposes. The results and stories told of these exploits were sometimes rather startling.

The early telescopes were simply long tubes formed from flat stock into the round, with an optical system. The reticule was fixed solidly in the scope tube and was focused at infinity. In many cases the mounts, which were simply means by which the scope was fixed to the barrel, were rigid and became part of the gun. In other cases such as a "Schlotter" percussion rifle I recently examined, the rear mount was a ring attached to a threaded shank which could be moved up and down for elevation. There was no windage adjustment, just elevation.

Some of the early manufacturers of telescopes were Whitworth, of England; William Malcolm, Syracuse, N. Y.; Lawson C. Cummins, Montpelier, Vt.; Milton B. Pierce of Rural Manufacturing Co., 44 North Fourth St., Philadelphia, Pa.; American Rifle Telescope Co., Buffalo, N.Y.; and Cataract Tool & Optical Co. of Buffalo, N. Y. A. O. Niedner made some scopes as did other riflesmiths. John W. Sidle, 1029 Filbert St., Philadelphia, Pa. also made fine scopes that were achromatic.

The Cataract Tool & Optical Co. of Buffalo, N. Y. was purchased by the J. Stevens Arms and Tool Company in 1901. Scopes offered prior to 1901 were made for Stevens by this company. After 1901 the manufacture of the telescopes was consolidated at the Chicopee Falls plant under the supervision of F. L. Smith who had been Cataract's manager.

Stevens mounts had both windage and elevation, and the shock of recoil was absorbed by the sliding tube just as our target telescopes today. Pistol scopes were offered with long eye relief. Stevens pioneered in wide angle lenses which increased the viewable field.

In 1907 Stevens introduced a variable scope from 6 to 11x magnification. Special reticules were also produced.

The nostalgic memories of collectors and shooters dwell on the long scopes which were in many instances Stevens' cheapest offering. It may be well to have a little nostalgia, but if you want to shoot these old rifles, get the best modern target scope you can afford; for if you can't see it, you can't hit it! The ocular system in the old scopes were good in their day, but then so was the "Model T."

Shortly before World War I Stevens sold its telescopic business to the Lyman Gun Sight Co. and so ended their venture into the scope business.

Winchester Repeating Arms Co. began making a tube type target telescope called the A5 in 1909. Workmanship was of the highest order, but the lens design was impractical. Although the scope was not entirely satisfactory it enjoyed a substantial sale and popularity. In 1928 Winchester discontinued the manufacture of the A5, and sold the entire operation to the Lyman Gun Sight Co.

The Lyman 5A scope was the redesigned Winchester A5. The Lyman 438 Field telescope and the 422 Expert were the old Stevens scopes.

Wollensak and Mossberg scopes were also tube type and very similar to the Stevens and the 438 and 422 of Lyman.

One of the most popular and exacting telescopes used by Schuetzen shooters was the Malcolm, and so it might be interesting to review briefly the story of the man William Malcolm.

William Malcolm was born at Sullivan, New York on October 13, 1823. He died at Syracuse, New York July 12, 1900.

The Malcolm family originally emigrated to the United States from Scotland. William Malcolm, senior, invested money in a large gunpowder manufacturing company and made a fortune from his investment.

After William junior's birth, the senior member of the family began to plan his son's life and decided that his son should be a professional man and add intellectual attainment to the family's material wealth.

As usual in family situations like this, things didn't work out as the proud father hoped. Young William was interested in the mechanics of things and was having success in the manufacture of firearms at the time his father died.

In spite of all his responsibilities he continued to study optical systems as a secondary interest. His first successful accomplishment was reported to be a telescope "with which he could see knot holes in a board at a distance of four miles from where he was experimenting."

As a result of his continued experiments he developed a telescope that did not require a constant refocusing, but had a "universal" focus.

Although his telescopic discoveries became known all over the world, he did not reveal his methods or secrets to anyone. Malcolm's scopes were individually and painstakingly made;

the result was that the enterprise never became a financial success, although many "scientists" of the day called his breakthrough the work of a genius.

His work, although known to gun enthusiasts for his rifle telescopes, was used in astronomical observatories the world over. United States, Russia, England, and Italy used Malcolm telescopes on heavy field guns with success.

During the early years of his work Malcolm ground his own lenses; later he ordered them from France and as manufacturing methods improved in the United States he was able in later years to turn to lenses made in this country.

During his own time, although he was recognized for his optical scientific contributions, he never became famous. Personally he was quiet and a self-absorbed individual although shooters who visited him spoke highly of his genteel and scholarly attitude. Individually he was held in very high regard by those who knew him. Oddly enough, the scientists of Europe knew more about him than did those in the United States. His secrets and knowledge were never transmitted to anyone else, and so all the work of his lifetime was lost to the world when he died.

It was said in a disparaging way "that he lacked the generous spirit that would find satisfaction in sharing with the world the discoveries that could confer benefits on the human race." After William Malcolm's death the Malcolm Rifle Telescope Company was carried on by others at Auburn, N. Y., but dropped out of the business after World War II.

Malcolm telescopes were made for rifle use before the Civil War, and during the war Malcolm, Mogg, and Sidle were the principal suppliers of rifle telescopes to the Union forces. The Confederate forces relied heavily on the Whitworth telescopes made for the Whitworth sniping rifles. The English telescopes were shorter than the U. S. made ones. The telescopes were not made by Whitworth, but by various optical makers to Whitworth's exacting specifications.

The best of the American telescopes were undoubtedly Malcolm's and the westward movement coupled with the war experience continued the demand for Malcolm instruments. The open country of the west encouraged the use of the telescopes, and an old issue of *Shooting and Fishing* records the fact that of a successful band of mountain men using muzzle loaders, all used Malcolm telescopes. Later it was written that the hunters had discarded the muzzle loaders and had 1874 Sharps rifles fitted with the best Malcolm scopes the hunters could get. All declared that once they had used a telescope sight they would not willingly go to any other sight.

With the muzzle loaders the long tube telescopes were carefully aligned with the bore, then brazed or sweated to the gun. The tubes were formed from flat stock and were usually ¾ inch diameter, although some were ½ inch. A Malcolm scope I have is a ⅝ inch diameter tube 10¼ inches long with a 3" eye relief.

Lens and reticule holders were placed into holders made of brass tubes; these then were placed into the steel tube and, after alignment, were held in place by screws from the outside of the tube.

Since the National Rifle Association (1871) was oriented to military shooting, the use of the telescope was forbidden. It was left to the Schuetzen rifle clubs to capitalize on the telescope's potential and to make good use of the instrument.

During the depression years of the 1930's the Malcolm Rifle Telescope Company of Auburn, N. Y. sold their product to shooters at a lower cost than their competitors — Lyman, Fecker, and Belding & Mull.

The No. 1 was offered in various magnifications from 4X to 10X. The lenses in this model were achromatic throughout. The No. 4 was made in 4X, and 8X.

Malcolm scopes were made in ¾" tube diameter and did not have enlarged eyepieces or enlarged objectives. The length of the tube could be 14, 16, 18, or 20 inches long.

The field of view at 100 yards for the 4X was 25.5 feet; 6X, 18 feet; and the 8X, 13.5 feet. The reticules included post, cross-hairs, and cross-hair with dot in center. The dot covered ⅓ inch at 25 yards. The cross-hairs were very fine. The eye relief on these old scopes was 1¾ inches, but 2½ inches could be had on request.

To change focus and correct parallax, a plate toward the front of the scope is moved back and forth as needed after loosening the single screw. The short plate at the rear is slid back and forth in the same manner to clear up the reticule and to take out parallax. The lenses were protected by metal caps threaded into either end of the tube.

The No. 1 scope was the best as far as resolution was concerned. As for the mountings, the tube was grooved for the Lyman 5A mounts.

The Malcolm "C" mounts were clamped to the tubes and did not permit the tube to slide. The front mount ring is fixed to a cross slide which provides the windage with the adjustment being made by screws on either side of the mount. To correct for windage move the scope in the opposite direction from the direction we are used to at the present time.

The rear mount has a yoke arrangement in which a square collar slides for elevation. The divisions on the elevation wheel are in 12's, and each mark represents 1 inch at 100 yards when the mounts are spaced 7½ inches apart. These mounts dovetail into the barrel, although some had standard bases fixed to the mounts which were screwed directly to the barrel. Some later ones were grooved for target bases which were narrower and lower than standard bases.

The 2½X and 3X were hunting scopes with a larger field and universal focus. At 100 yards the field of view was 45 and 34 feet respectively.

Some of these Malcolm scopes will be found with Stevens mounts and others with adaptations which permitted the use of Lyman and Winchester mounts. The mountings were determined by the shooter, for the telescopes were sold either with or without the Malcolm mounts.

Several letters of interest appear in the *American Field* such as the one in the April 3, 1886 issue, as follows:

"Telescope Sights for Pistols.—Syracuse, N.Y.—Editor American Field:—An article in your issue of February 20, by Algonquin, of Ottawa, Canada, contained some statements in regard to the accuracy of a rifle pistol with a thirteen-inch barrel. Now, if I am not in error a pistol with a barrel over twelve inches in length becomes a short gun. Be that as it may, I am glad to hear of one friend of the pistol — an arm that I have owned and used for over forty years, more or less. The accuracy of the shooting with this short arm is greatly augmented by the use of a carefully and scientifically made telescope sight. The difficulty of holding a short arm is apparent to all, and a sight which detects imperfect holding is a benefit. Of course a poorly or unscientifically made telescope is worthless on any rifle and not as good as a globe and bead. A few years since, I attached the best telescope I could make to a pistol made by the late Wm. Billinghurst, of Rochester, N. Y. The barrel was eleven and seven-eights inches in length and .32-caliber. It had swedge patent muzzle and cap starter and was a muzzle-loader. Soon after the telescope was attached, Mr. John Showt, the owner, fired it at 230 yards at rest, eleven shots in succession, striking a six-inch ring nine times. The entire eleven shots gave a string measure of twenty-six and three-eighths inches from the center of the ball hole to the center of the target. This performance is not an exceptional one and can be approximated to or excelled on any fair or still day.   Wm. Malcolm"

In another instance the discussion regarding adjustable mounts became quite heated. This discussion was originally set off by a letter of January 9, 1886 when a writer wrote, "I do not see why one of suitable construction could not be easily mounted on the side of a rifle and arranged so as to oscillate on a central trunnion to give different elevations."

In answer to this inquiry Milton P. Pierce who had made telescopes for the muzzle loaders had this to say on January 30, 1886:

". . . .with reference to oscillating telescope sights attached to the side of rifles. Experiments of that kind were made here over twenty years ago, during our civil war. Several officers had excellent rifles thus fitted, the work being done in the most thorough manner by a mathematical instrument establishment in this city, which has already been noted for the excellence of its work. So far as accuracy was concerned the plan proved a failure. A telescope sight must be attached in the most rigid manner possible; that shown in the advertising columns of the American Field has thus far given the most satisfactory results. It is impracticable to make this attachment upon many of the breech-loading rifles, but nearly as good an attachment for breech-loaders is practically the same as shown in the engraving (minus the lug or ear screws, which fasten the telescope to the elevating post) with a sliding guide attached by dove-tail just forward of the lock and with a set-screw passing through this slide and with a sleeve attachment similar to the one over the small of the stock. This middle attachment must of course coincide with the end attachments; then, when the telescope is properly aligned and the elevation properly adjusted, the set-screw referred to can be screwed fast and the telescope is thus held rigid to the barrel, while the rear attachment, although not screwed fast, serves to steady the telscope as well as to indicate whether it has been moved by concussion in firing. I fitted up and used an attachment of this kind over twenty years ago, which gave good satisfaction. The attachments shown in the engraving, I prefer to all others where their use is practicable, as it is on all muzzle-loaders.

Milton P. Pierce"

Another comment in the same issue was from the American Rifle Telescope Co. of Buffalo, New York, and stated that an attachment was available as suggested by the reader's letter. This attachment was "a self acting adjustment to compensate for the lateral movement necessary in elevation. It is a perfect success and can be attached to any rifle in five minutes."

A letter written on April 10, 1886 sums up the whole problem which is still valid today.

"Telescope Sights for Off-Hand Shooting.—Warren, O.—Editor American Field:—The subject of sights for rifles seems to me very far from being exhausted and needs much discussion among riflemen. It is hard for us to give up old notions and adopt new ideas. Besides, the intent and tendency of those who should be interested is to discourage any improvement. I mean by this that many clubs bar all sights but open sights; others improve a little and allow the globe and peep sights to be used; but all bar telescopes. Why is this? In my opinion there is no sight yet invented which is good enough. We are told that the telescope sight for off-hand shooting is impractical and one "cannot hold still enough." True, the telescope shows all errors and unsteadiness; but how can one expect to shoot closer than he can hold? If the sight is an advantage and therefore should not be tolerated, then take off all sights; the skill, or luck, will be greater should you make good shooting. Our Creedmoor friends reluctantly allow globe and peep sights to be used; but at 1,000 yards the bead would cover a barn and their shooting is correspondingly accurate. There is no practice as beneficial as sighting with the telescope off-hand; the eye, hand and finger soon learn to work together. Cost is one objection, it is true; but a poor gun is dear at any price and the best is the cheapest.

Buckeye"

Chapter 20

HINTS ON LOADING THE SINGLE SHOT RIFLE

When Schuetzen rifle shooting was popular in the United States during the 1880's and 1890's and to a lesser degree up until 1916, the business man, the professional man, and the working man could carry the few things we call accessories in a small bag, and with his fine single shot rifle could go to the range by trolley or carriage and enjoy a full day of relaxing shooting.

The accent during the Schuetzen days was on offhand shooting, and the usual range was 200 yards. Depending upon where one lived a fine Pope, Niedner, Schoyen, or Peterson rifle with the accessories was much less than one would spend on a first class rifle with its accessories of today. These fine old single shot rifles demand premium prices as collectors' items, but in the days when they when they were made they were not a luxury item but rather a precision instrument far beyond what the factories with their tolerances and hasty fitting could provide. The makers and the users of the fine rifles of yesteryear were interested in accuracy and the enjoyment of using a fine instrument.

The ammunition and method of shooting the rifles cost on the average one cent a shot. Today a fine target rifle will cost many times the cost of the Schuetzen rifles, and the ammunition thirty to fifty times what the single shot rifle shooter had to spend.

To the average modern shooter the tremendous care and attention to detail necessary to make these old rifles shoot becomes irksome, and as a result many of these fine rifles have become relics to be admired and talked of but seldom to be used. It is my hope that the reader will be inspired to try some of the old methods and to find the enjoyment and satisfaction in forgetting the hurried demand to shoot and be gone, and instead perhaps find a little of the enjoyment of those from the past.

Some of the old fine rifles have had over 25,000 rounds through them and yet today are capable of the same fine accuracy, if the shooter is willing to forget speed and will use the soft lead bullets. If you want to use jacketed bullets and high velocities why go to the old guns; use the modern ones. This was the theme Ned Roberts used in my correspondence with him years ago, and it is still true today and will be in the future.

The Schuetzen shooting was popular among civilian clubs but was ridiculed by the U. S. Army because the use of the palm rest, the hip rest position, the false muzzle for loading; the weight of the rifle and the set triggers were impractical for military use. Today, after all the intervening years, rifle competition is beginning to break away from this army concept and we find heavy rifles, palm rests, adustable butt plates, etc., being used once again.

Many of the old percussion rifles, after which the cartridge Schuetzen rifle was patterned, were undoubtedly designed by the Swiss or Tyrolean rifle makers during the nineteenth century. These rifles were designed as offhand rifles for shooting at 200 and 220 yards. The 220 yards was 40 rods or 200 meters, a unit of measure used in those countries.

Since the primary purpose of these rifles was accuracy, the weight, caliber, and triggers were not restricted. The rifle was made to the individual requirements of the rifleman who could modify it as far as stock, loading, etc., if he thought it would improve the accuracy of the rifle.

The rules which developed in this country for the cartridge Schuetzen clubs prohibited the use of a metal cased bullet, and as smokeless powder became available some of them even restricted its use except as a priming charge for the black powder. As to who developed the method of loading duplex loads for cleaner shooting there is some debate, but in any case practically all the Schuetzen shooters used this method until the advent of the old Dupont "Schuetzen" powder and the improved powders which followed. In any case, the bullets were always restricted to the lead bullet whether it was cast, swaged and whether lubricated or paper patched.

The term we use today is not "Schuetzen rifle" but free rifle, in that the rifle has been freed of all restrictions and the thumbhole and other innovations are attempts to provide more individual precision free of regulations which limit the effort. Like today's free rifles the old single shot rifles were heavy barreled, and the rifleman could not hold them steady by using an extended forearm as in military shooting. However, by pressing the left elbow (if right handed) close to the body and resting it on the hip bone and by supporting the rifle on the finger tips and thumb, the rifle could be kept on the target more easily. Men who have short arms in proportion to their bodies found that by dropping a device down from the forearm called a "palm rest" they could also assume this position and shoot in a more steady position. Dr. W. G. Hudson, one of the famous expert shots of the 1880's, did not use the palm rest on any of his rifles. He did, however, use the "hip rest" position and rested the rifle on his extended fingers and thumb of his left hand.

These early rifles had shallow grooves; as a result the early Remington and Sharps rifles perform better with paper patched bullets. The Ballard rifle, made in later years by J. M. Marlin, had a deeper groove depth and so used the naked lubricated lead bullet more successfully.

When breech loading rifles were first introduced, the manufacturers felt that no rifle less than .40 caliber would give good accuracy at 200 yards. The "Creedmoor" rifles of Remington and Sharps were both originally made in .44/90/550 bottleneck center fire. Later match rifles used various .40, .44, or .45 bottlenecked cartridges as well as the straight taper cases. All used heavy charges of black powder and a paper patched bullet. The paper patched bullet is seated lightly in the case without crimping. After firing each shot, the bore was cleaned with a wet or soapy patch, then dried with clean dry patches. Once the shooter found the best method of cleaning his rifle after each shot he never varied the procedure; being very careul to use the same each time. Late in the 1880's smokeless powders were developed, and the single shot rifle shooters adopted the method of duplex loading. This duplex load consisted of not more than 10% of the load in smokeless powder dropped into the case, then the rest filled with black powder. This is still a good load to use and one of the best priming charges is with Dupont #4227 I.M.R. powder. For example, we might use the .45/70 cartridge. Set the powder measure to 5 or 6 grains on the scale of the measure. If using an Ideal, this gives a BULK measure, not weight! Use the measure to drop in your smokeless charge, then use a second measure to drop the black powder to fill the case. Many old shooters used a card wad placed over the powder charge, more to hold it in place than anything else. This method requires a wad cutter that will cut a wad about .458. The best material to use for the wad is old postal cards or something of similar thickness and firmness. The wad is seated over the powder with the fingers.

The best powder measure to use for the duplex load is the old Ideal Number 6 which was made with a double chamber expressly for this purpose. These old measures, however, cannot be readily found. To give good loading with black powder I prefer a long drop tube on the powder measure - either a 10 or 12 inch brass tube being preferred.

The method of using duplex loads was called "dirty shooting" because the barrel didn't have to be cleaned after every shot. In my 1873 Springfield I have found that even with this loading I get my best accuracy by cleaning after each shot; so again this points up the need to find out what *your* rifle needs and stick to it.

To breech seat your bullets directly into the rifle, either make a bullet seater like the old "Ideal" seater or for simplicity use the "plugged case" method. To make a plugged case seater, get a wooden dowel which is a close fit in the cartridge case you are going to use. Force the wooden dowel completely to bottom of the case and cut it off one-sixteenth of an inch longer than the case. The seater is now ready to use. Insert the lubricated bullet into the chamber and put in the seater, close the action forcing the bullet into the grooves. Open the action, take out the seater, put in the primed case with the powder and wad, and the rifle is ready to fire.

A rifle must have the following factors just right before it will shoot well: the bullet must be of the right shape, weight, size, temper (ratio of tin to lead), and be lubricated with a combination that works best in that particular bore. If you are going to use smokeless powder, then you must experiment to find the right load. Once you have found the right combination, stick with it! I experimented with a low wall Winchester single shot in .25/20 Stevens for over five years before I found the right combination and now when my shooting is good I can get unbelieveably small groups with this rifle time after time. On the other hand, I know of a rifleman who is never satisfied and is constantly changing one factor or another of his shooting without keeping a record or analyzing his changes. The result is that he always has an alibi but rarely a good target. In any case his conversation is always enthusiastic because of a proposed change, but his targets are somewhat lacking in the evidence. In the event you test a load, record the results and with the record list the information about the bullet and results. Keep these records! They are valuable for analysis and will keep you from making the same mistakes or wandering without reason.

The following letter appeared in the *American Field* of April 17, 1886, page 375, which may prove of interest to the reader:

Minneapolis, Minn.

EDITOR AMERICAN FIELD:—I wish to call attention to the scores of the Minneapolis team of two men, published in this issue in another place, not for the excellence of the shooting so much as to notice the conditions and ammunition. The ammunition was all prepared by myself, that Mr. Maudlin using being brought to the range all loaded, while mine was loaded as fast as fired, but one or two shells being used. Sixty grains

of Hazard FG powder was used, and a 420 grain grooved bullet,
cast and lubricated by myself, from old bullets picked up at the
butts mostly long range and containing 1 to 11 of tin. They
were cast in a .45 government mold, made by the Winchester
Co., and shot from a Remington special military .44 caliber rifle,
made especially for patched bullets. The lubricant was a mixture
of cosmoline, stearine and white wax.

But what would seem to my friend Van Dyke impossible,
is that they were shot from a government shell which is about
⅝ of an inch shorter than the chamber, and the bullet seated
deep in the shell so that the point of the bullet did not come
even with the back end of the rifling and neither rifle was cleaned throughout the match. It is the ammunition I have used ex-
clusively for the past six months, and I can call my shots as well
as with any rifle and ammunition I ever used. Of course no
claim is made as to the superiority of the short shell; it is the
the only one I could get in which I could seat the bullets, but
it shows that the horrors of seating a bullet into the shell and
slamming it into the groove have been greatly overestimated.

I have never tried a rest at 200 yards to test the extreme
accuracy of the ammunition, as I am not an advocate of that
style of shooting; but I have made 48 out of a possible 50 on
the Creedmoor target twice and 45 to 47 a number of times in
the past six months. Mr. Maudlin thinks he could nearly if
not quite equal his scores made with the match rifle where the
bullet is placed in groove and clean after each shot. In justice to
Mr. Maudlin I will say that the rifle he shot was strange to him
and the sights could not be adjusted and he had to hold ten or
twelve inches below the bullseye in order to hit it.

In military or "dirty gun" shooting much more care should
be taken to have everything just right than when the rifle is
cleaned after each shot. My conclusions from six months or more
trial of different kinds of charges and close observation is about
as follows: A small charge of coarse, moist burning powder (not
necessarily a high grade, costly powder), say 60 grains for a .44
or .45 caliber, and a rather heavy, hard and tight fitting bullet
— the 405 or 500 grain government give about equal results,
but on account of less recoil, I now use the lightest. I do not
simply breathe through the barrel, but spit through it swiftly
two or three times right after shooting, then set it down and
let the powder crust sack. There is no danger of getting too
much moisture in the barrel if the barrel is held perpendicular,
for the surplus will run out. I am speaking now of lubricated
bullets only; with patched bullets, I do not know how much
moisture is necessary. With an international match staring us

in the face, all should be learned about dirty gun shooting that can be, and a free exchange of experiences and results of observations can but lead to real benefit.

It seems a little strange that nearly all the long-range men of our rifle club use .44 caliber Remington bullets in .45 caliber Ballard rifles, while I use a .45 government bullet in a .44 Remington rifle at 200 yards; but I do not think there is the difference in the calibers that the number would indicate. In long-range shooting we use a loose fitting bullet and depend on the heavy powder charge upsetting the bullet and making it take the grooves; with the light powder charge which will not upset the hard bullet much if any, it must be so tight that the lands are stamped into the bullet even when pushed through with a rod.

C. M. Skinner.

Chapter 21

LEAD BULLETS AND LUBRICANTS

About 1879 the .38/55 C. F. cartridge was developed especially for the Ballard rifle made by the J. M. Marlin Company. This cartridge was found to be especially accurate at 200 yards, and the Schuetzen shooters quickly adopted this cartridge in preference to the .40, .44, and .45 caliber arms. The .38/55 originally used a 330 grain paper patched bullet. Later the lubricated bullet was used in the same weight. The caliber was popular both because of the lessened recoil and the fine accuracy it gave. However, it was but a few more years and the .32/40 cartridge, again developed for the Marlin and Ballard rifles, became popular for the same reason the .38/55 replaced the .40's, .44's, and .45's. The .32/40 used a 185 or 200 grain bullet either paper patched or lubricated as the shooter desired.

Later H. M. Pope developed a .33 caliber using a 195 or 218 grain lubricated bullet which was as accurate as the .32/40 and on a windy day was less affected by the crosswinds due to the heavier bullet.

About 1900-01 the .28/30 Stevens cartridge with a 136 grain lubricated Pope bullet became popular for 200 yard shooting.

The .25/20, .25/21, and .25/25 Stevens cartridges all proved popular, but the serious shooters for the most part stuck with the .38/55, the .32/40, the Pope .33, and the .28/30.

The rifles with false muzzles have the bullet seated from the muzzle and pushed all the way back to about 1/16 of an inch in front of the case. While this method of placing the bullet in the rifle slows the firing, it does improve accuracy a great deal in a rifle fired with black powder: many riflemen including Ned Roberts have found that when smokeless powders are used the muzzle loading of the bullet makes no difference in the accuracy.

This does not mean that breech seating the bullet through the chamber and into the lands does not improve accuracy, for quite the contrary, this method invariably improves accuracy with one of these rifles. After seating the bullet, the case with the powder is then inserted into the chamber in the normal manner, and the arm is ready for firing.

The finest of the old time makers, Schoyen, Peterson, Zischang, Pope, and others, always furnished a complete outfit with the rifles they made. These outfits included a bullet mould, bullet lubricating pump, a re and de capper, a powder measure,

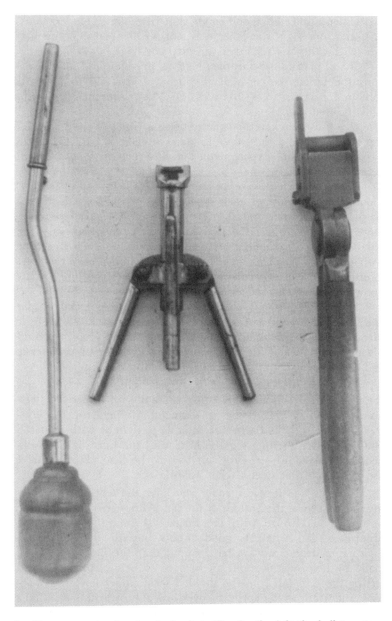

Loading accessories for the single shot rifle. On the left the bullet seater; center, Pope re-and de-capper; on the right a Pope double cut off mold. Schoyen also made similar molds.

and, if ordered, a false muzzle, bullet starter and bullet seating rod.

The best load for your rifle can only be found by careful experimentation. The good single shot rifles are like opera stars, and what one likes the other may not, so planned experimentation with complete records is necessary.

If you plan to use a duplex load of smokeless and black powders, the bullet temper will vary from 1 part tin to 30 parts lead to 1 part tin to 50 parts of lead. Try different tempers to find the best one.

If you use smokeless powders you may find you need a bullet hardness from 1 part tin to 15 parts lead to 1 part tin to 25 parts lead. Again experimentation and actual shooting will determine the right one.

When shooting or experimenting with the lead temper, shoot 10 or 20 shots of each type of hardness. Pick a load and keep both the load and lubricant constant for all these tests. Once you have found the best bullet, then you may vary the type of lubricant, keeping records all the time! Then the same with powders. In other words, reduce the number of variables to one. When you experiment and vary all three you don't really know what has resulted or why.

In casting bullets I have used the old lead pot and dipper and have made good bullets. Then I changed to a Potter electric furnace (they made one of the first), and today I use a Mould Master from Ideal. The way you cast is a matter of preference and experience will make the changes as you develop.

When the furnace or pot is at the right temperature and the lead is all freely melted, I flux the pot with a piece of beeswax about 1/4 or 5/16 inches in diameter. Simply drop the beeswax into the pot and when it fumes up, light it with a match and while it is burning stir the lead until the burning has stopped; then skim off the dross on top of the lead. To do this I use a common flat steel kitchen spatula.

In using an electric furnace you have the advantage of taking the lead from the bottom of the pot. Although a mould guide or rest is sold to go with the furnace, I find this more of a hindrance than a help to good bullets, but this may be an individual matter. I always have found that the best bullets are made by holding the mold an inch or so below the spout and letting the lead fall into the mold. I seem to get fewer air bubbles, and I allow the sprue to overflow almost a half a bullet's weight and in this way I have a large sprue which prevents airholes in the base of the bullet.

I use a piece of soft fir or pine as a knock off stick to hit the sprue cutter after the sprue has "set." The bullets are dumped onto a piece of plywood about 12" by 18" which has been padded with several thicknesses of felt.

After casting for a while I return the sprue cuts to the pot and try to keep the bullets in an order as cast. When the bullets are cold enough to handle, examine any for imperfections and if any are found, return them to the pot. As you find time, weigh the bullets and group them from the standard + one grain, standard, — one grain. These bullets if all the same weight will group equally well, but all will group differently than the standard weight. You can't see air bubbles in a bullet, and and anyone who tells you he casts bullets without them is avoiding reality. Many old time shooters swaged their bullets to remove these air bubbles, but in any case weighing the bullet is necessary for the finest shooting of small groups.

As for primers - this seems to be a matter of preference with various brands being used and staunchly defended by the individual shooter. Some shooters weigh their primers and reject any that vary from the standard. Personally, I have not found this necessary, especially with the quality controls maintained by the U. S. ammunition manufacturing companies.

The problem of finding the proper bullet lubricant can also be frustrating. If you like to experiment, here are some tried and reliable formulas furnished by various persons and publications which were active during the old Schuetzen days.

Here is the Kephart lubricant as given by "Arms and the Man." 3 parts Ozocerite wax and 2 parts vaseline. Waxes should be melted and mixed in a double boiler so they will not scorch or burn.

John Kaufmann, an old time Schuetzen rifleman now deceased, used beeswax and vaseline, half and half. He said it was as good as any.

A. Sizer, of West Virginia, used the following combination in his fine bench-rest shooting: 3 parts Bayberry wax, 1 part beeswax, and 1 part vaseline, and soften with tallow or more vaseline if the weather is too cold.

The following is the Pope lubricant: beeswax, 2 oz.; bayberry wax, 4 oz.; mutton tallow, 6 oz.; steam cylinder oil, 2 oz.; Acheson graphite #1340, 170 grs. or two heaping teaspoons.

Here is Leopold's Standard Lubricant #245 which he put on the market years ago: 4½ oz. Japan wax; 9 oz. Degras Stearin; (beef or mutton tallow should do as well); 1½ oz. Ozocerite; 55/100 or ½ oz. caustic soda and rosin, each, boiled in ½ pint of water and mixed with the melted waxes, and boiled until the froth disappears. Mr. Sizer wrote that this was a fine lubricant for warm weather but not for cold.

Leopold's lubricant #97 which he considered as good as any but too expensive to market: 16 oz. beeswax; 12 oz. bayberry wax; 8 oz. paraffin; 9 oz. spermaceti; 5 oz. beef tallow; 5 oz. lanolin (anhydrous) ; 2½ oz. white castile soap. Melt and mix together and cook in a double boiler for one-half hour or until the white froth on top disappears. This is a saponified lubricant like #245, and it is difficult to remelt.

Here is the lubricant Abel Merchant used. Two other old time riflemen and experimenters said it was "par excellence." 3 parts tallow, mutton or beef; 1 part bayberry wax, (Japan wax or beeswax) ; 1 part vaseline. Temper this lubricant according to the weather. With some, it does better on the soft side using a bullet I part tin to 16 of lead. Castor oil may be tried in place of vaseline. Sometimes it seems to have a lot of drag to it and may not work as well.

Several modern day shooters of the American Single Shot Rifle Association have also developed successful lubricants as follows:

M. W. Manny and R. Hill: 1 oz. beef or mutton tallow; 2 oz. ozocerite wax; 2 oz. Japan wax; 5 oz. beeswax; 1 oz. steam cylinder oil.

H. Beveridge: 2 oz. yellow vaseline, 4 oz. mutton tallow, 10 oz. Japan wax, 6 oz. beeswax, 6 oz. crude Ozocerite.

The purpose of lubricating a bullet is to prevent leading of the bore. A paper patched bullet is cylindrical and the entire bearing surface is protected by the paper, so no leading can result if these bullets are used although some shooters did place a thin disc of lubricant over the wad and under the bullet.

To make sheets of lubricant for wads, melt the lubricant in water using a flat large cake pan. Get a smooth round bottle and fill with cold water. When the lubricant is hot, revolve the bottle along the surface of the water the lubricant is in. This will put a thin film on the bottle. Keep building up this film by making successive passes with the bottle, giving it a chance to cool between times so that the bottle does not get so warm it melts the lubricant. When the lubricant is to the desired thickness, split it lengthwise with a knife, cut off the top and bottom sections, and you have a rectangular sheet left. Return the scrap lubricant to the pan for remelting. Keep the sheet lubricant between sheets of waxed paper. Cut the lubricant with some kind of a wad cutter to fit the case. A. O. Niedner, the noted riflesmith and Schuetzen shooter, taught me this years ago, and I have found this the best and easiest method of producing wax wad material. This wax wad should be placed over the card wad that holds the powder in. The best card wads are made from material about the thickness and firmness of a postal card.

Other lubricants which have been used in the past are as follows:

1. Three parts tallow to one part beeswax.
2. Four parts tallow to one of beeswax.
3. One part tallow, four parts beeswax.
4. Japan wax.
5. Sperm oil and beeswax - this must be used at once; no good for cartridges to be loaded and used later.
6. Three parts tallow, two parts beeswax; spindle oil to give a salve like texture; graphite can be added.
7. Beeswax four parts, cylinder (or heavy) oil one part.
8. Walnut Hill - three parts mutton tallow, one part wax. Add a teaspoonful of plumbago to a pint of the melted material. If it proves too hard upon cooling, add sperm oil.

For the tallow go to the meat counter and get the trimmings from the meat. Be sure it is not salted. Trim off all the meat scraps and use the pure tallow. Put your electric skillet on low heat and let the tallow simmer; pour it off as it melts, and continue the rendering until all is melted out. I have stored mine in waxed refrigerator containers, and it keeps for years.

Formulas for wax wads only are as follows:

Leopold - 5 oz. Japan wax, 5 oz. beeswax, 2 oz. Ozocerite, 3 or 4 teaspoonsful of Acheson Graphite #1340.

Donaldson-2 oz. rosin, 4 oz. beeswax, 3 oz. Japan wax, 2 oz. tallow, 2 oz. Acheson Graphite #38. (Barrel problems have been reported because of the use of rosin) .

Roberts - 6 oz. Ozocerite, 2 oz. graphite, 2 oz. beeswax, 3 oz. tallow.

Watkyns & Sweany - 16 oz. beeswax, 4 oz. graphite, 4 oz. castor oil.

Sharpe - 4 grams Oildag, 2 grams castor oil, 4 grams beeswax, 12 grams Japan wax, 1 gram petrolatum.

Ozocerite is a mineral wax product from Siberia and is used by electrotyping businesses, so this might be a source of supply.

When lubricating bullets without sizing them, either fill a shallow cake or pie pan with bullets, set on end, and pour the lubricant into the pan; or heat the lubricant and set the bullets into the lubricant. In either case, let the lubricant cool, then push the bullets through the lubricant block by pushing on the point end with the fingers. The grooves should be uniformly filled with this method.

Chapter 22

PAPER PATCH BULLETS

I have heard collectors enthuse over the old paper patch cartridges and have heard remarks about paper patching being a lost art. It might be to modern shooters, but certainly it is not complicated. The practice is tedious, monotonous, and time consuming; but it is not a lost art! Anyone, by following directions and taking his time, can make paper patched bullets that are very creditable.

First, the problem of where are you going to get a slug mold to cast the bullet. This is a problem! I have found several of the Ideal molds at gun shows recently, but this is probably unusual. I have also found Ideal and Winchester regular molds that have been made to cast a smooth slug. The simplest method I know of right now is to buy an Ideal slug mold of the correct size and take out the end plug and either turn a nose point in the plug or have some one do it, and presto, you have a perfect cylindrical slug bullet ready for patching! These slug molds are made for casting the core which home bullet makers use to fill the jacket of the jacketed bullets they make. I have converted several of these molds and have had no problems. I have found that the instructions given in the Ideal Handbook No. 7, published in 1896 by the Ideal Manufacturing Co., New Haven, Conn., is as complete as needed.

"Patched bullets are smooth, without grooves. They are from three to six thousandths of an inch smaller than is required for the rifle; the diameter is increased to the size desired by having a thin paper patch rolled around the bullet, covering about two-thirds of the bullet from the base up. The paper is of fine strong texture, similar to bank-note paper. It is specially prepared for this purpose, and is made in different thicknesses, which are known to the manufacturers of ammunition as extra-thin, medium and thick. The extra-thin is about one and one-half thousandths in thickness and there is an increase of about one-half thousandth in each succeeding size; thus shooters wishing to increase or decrease the diameter of their bullets can do so by selecting the proper thickness of paper. There is a difference of opinion relative to the advantage or superiority of patched bullets over grooved, yet for hunting or military purposes the grooved ball is generally preferred, as such ammunition can be carried and exposed to wet weather without injury, while a part of the patch being exposed is liable to get wet and injured so as to impair its accuracy. Still, for fine target-shooting, the patched bullet properly handled is, without doubt, preferable.

How to Patch Bullets. The ordinary factory-patched bullets have *two* laps of paper around them. The patch is cut in length so that the ends do not lap over but almost butt up to each other. The regular patch is cut on an angle so that the joining of the laps will not be parallel with the rifling or the axis of the bullet, thus holding the patch securely over both points of the lap.

How to Fit a Patch. First cut a strip of paper the width desired; have it long enough to lap *three* times; roll firmly about the body of bullet; have edge of paper square and even with base of bullet; when so rolled, hold point of bullet from you and with the point of a sharp knife cut through all thicknesses of paper *except* about a sixteenth of an inch at the base; commence cutting from the point toward the base, scribing the angle desired around the circumference of the bullet. When unrolled the *two inner full-sized pieces* that are held together by the uncut part will represent, *when put together,* the shape and length of patch desired, except the cutting off of about one sixty-fourth of an inch in length, preserving the same angle, thus preventing the possibility of the ends lapping over. When the patch is found to be correct, a piece of sheet metal can be filed up the shape and size, to be used as a template or pattern to cut others. Before putting the patches on it will be well to dampen them between two wet cloths so as to take the crisp out of the paper. This will also cause it to lap snugly to the ball and help in the matter of closing the paper over at the base, which when perfectly dried will have shrunk firmly to the bullet. *Do not* make patches too wet, or use mucilage or any sticky substance, for patches *must leave bullet* clean at departure from rifle.

How to Roll on Patch. Lay the patch on a smooth board or table with the point of angles toward and from you; have *point* of angle toward you to the *right;* let the whole of the angle project over the edge of the board or table (this will leave the point of patch free, not stuck down to the table;) then place the bullet squarely upon the patch, (base to the left,) letting as much of the paper project beyond the base as you desire. The angle projecting toward you can then be lapped up over the bullet. When in that in that position, place the forefinger upon the point of patch and bullet, and with a forward push roll the bullet up on the patch. You will soon perceive whether you are rolling it on true; if not, roll back, readjust the bullet, and try again. A little practice will soon enable you to acquire the art so that you will do it correctly every time. This is the method of patching bullets at the ammunition factories. This work is done by girls, who become expert, some of them patching over twelve thousand per day.

The regular patched bullets have a cavity at the base. When patch is rolled on, the paper should project about *two-thirds* of the diameter of the ball and the projecting paper is twisted over the base, and pressed into the cavity. With the flat base bullet (without cavity) allow the patch to project only *one-third* of the diameter of the ball and turn the edge of paper over inward, and press the base of ball, when so patched, flat upon a table, and the result will be one-third of the base of the ball bare.

The Chasé Patch (or single lap.) Cut the paper the width that you desire to cover the ball. Lap *once only* and have ends square, butting up together, joined lengthwise of bullet, edge of paper flush with base of bullet. The method of patching is to simply roll the patch (after size is determined) tube shape and insert it into the ball-seater. Allow the paper to project beyond the muzzle of the shell (on ball-seater;) square up the patch by gently pressing it against the plunger; insert the bullet within the patch and press ball and patch both against plunger; place in chamber of rifle and with plunge seat ball and patch together into the barrel in advance of shell to depth required. (*Patches dry and crisp.*) This method of loading has scored the best records that have ever been made. It, of course, is of no value to the hunter or military shooter, but demonstrates what may be done in the way of accuracy with a single-shot rifle under the very best possible conditions. In seating patched bullets *in the shell,* some use a thin wad over the powder, then a disc of lubrication, on top of which is seated the bullet. Others seat the bullet on top of powder without wad or lubrication, wiping after each shot. Experience must decide these points for each shooter.

Expanded shells will not, of course, hold the standard bullets securely so as to prevent them dropping out, which is very annoying. Such shells should be resized with the Ideal Re-sizing Tools. The practice of increasing the diameter of the bullets, by using thicker patch paper or an extra lap, is entirely wrong, as the bullets *should not* be above the correct diameter for the bore of the rifle whether they fit the shells or not. It is the *barrel and not the shells* that the bullets should fit properly to get good results. If your rifle expands the shells and you desire to shoot patched bullets, or uncrimped shells and grooved bullets, and have them held securely, so as to carry the ammunition, the *shells must be re-sized*. By reserving a new shell that has never been *crimped or shot* you will have a reference gauge that will show you whether the shells that have been fired are expanded or not.

The well-known expert rifleman, Francis J. Rabbeth, (known to the shooting fraternity as "J. Francis") who has been doing such wonderful shooting at the rest-matches at Walnut Hill Range, near Boston, Mass., uses a patched bullet in a rifle chambered for the regular 38-55 cartridge. This bullet has a straight cylindrical body. It is composed of 1 part tin to 25 of lead, cast in a cylindrical adjustable mould, not swaged. He uses F. G. Hazard powder, 55 grains packed in his 38-55 everlasting shell with an Ideal Loading Flask, and uses no wads; bullets patched Chase method, (one thickness square patch,) thickness of patch two to two and one-fourth thousandths; bullets seated in chambers 1-32 ahead of shell with an Ideal Ballseater; cleans after each shot with a Fischer brush, *wet,* pushing it through with a rod having a snug-fitting wiping-rag attached. This rag is pushed clear through the barrel from the breech and drawn back; no second wiping. He uses no oil or lubricant. On July 18, 1891, Mr. Rabbeth performed the wonderful feat of placing fifteen successive shots into a two-inch ring at 200 yards, (recorded). The gentleman has kindly furnished us with the above statement as to how he loads and makes his bullets.

The straight cylindrical bullet has been proven, beyond a doubt, superior to the regular tapered bullet.

Bullets seated in the barrel with ball-seater should not be forced in too tight. Experience has proven that the standard diameter of the smooth ball with "Chase patch" (one lap of medium patch paper) is about the correct thing. This of course is not quite so snug a fit as the same ball with the two lap factory-patch."

Today the paper problem can be solved by using a very high grade bond paper with as high a rag content as you can get. 50 to 100 sheets of this material will last for years. To determine the thickness needed, measure the bore diameter by taking a lead bullet slightly larger than the hole of the bore and tap it into the bore with a hammer; don't hit the end of the barrel! Then take a steel rod just smaller than the diameter of the bore and push or tap the bullet through the bore. Catch the bullet as it comes out, and by using a micrometer measure the distance across the grooves on the bullet. This measurement is the bore diameter. Next, measure the slug you are going to use. The difference is the thickness of the paper you will need. If the measurement is .004, then the paper thickness will have to be .002; for the difference must be divided by two to take care of the size on *both* sides of the bullet.

The bore of the rifle must not have any roughness in it if you intend to shoot paper patches, for if there is the paper will tear, or hang up, on the spot and you will not get any accuracy. Shooting paper patches will shine a bore until it's like a mirror, and the longer you use them the better the bore seems to get. Early Remington, Sharps, and some of the others will shoot better with paper patched bullet than with lubricated ones if the bore is in good shape. If the bore is not smooth the paper patch will not be accurate, and only trying it out will indicate whether paper patched or lubricated bullets will shoot accurately.

Chapter 23

WHITNEY ARMS

The Whitney Arms Company was formed at New Haven, Connecticut in the heart of the firearms industry. The basis for the firearm was a patent issued March 21, 1871 to Eli Whitney.

The action is similar to the Remington rolling block action, and they are not usually found.

Later the Phoenix Breech Loader was manufactured. This action has a hinged flip flop breach block instead of a rolling block. These rifles are more easily found than are the rolling block types.

The rolling block rifle was made as a long and midrange target rifle with a vernier long stem tang sight and a globe front sight. A windgauge front sight was also offered as optional sighting equipment as was the front sight spirit level. The long range rifle was offered in .44 caliber with a 32 or 34 inch barrel. The mid range was in .40 caliber with a 30 or 32 inch barrel. This model was also offered in a .22 gallery model with a 24 inch barrel being the standard length.

The Phoenix action was offered in a Schuetzen .38 or .40 caliber barrel, a German pattern Schuetzen stock, vernier sights, and barrel length of either 30 or 32 inches. A gallery rifle in .22 caliber was also offered.

Both the Whitney and the Phoenix were offered in military models of .43 or .45 caliber. Sporting rifles were also offered in various calibers.

Later the Whitney Company manufactured the Burgess and the Kennedy repeating lever action rifles.

THE WHITNEY
Military, Sporting, Hunting and Target

Breech-Loading Rifles. Prices Reduced.

☞ For Accuracy, Long-Range, Penetrat'on, Simplicity of Construction, Durability, Ease of Manipulation, Material and Workmanship they are unsurpa sed. PHOENIX SPOkTING RIFLES AND SHOT-GUNS—We call especial attention to the improved Phœnix Sporting, Target and Saloon Rifles. They are the cheapest first-class rifles ever offered in the United States. Revolvers of various sizes, desirable in all respects, at extremely low prices
Send for Circulars, with reduced prices.
WHITNEY ARMS CO , New Haven, Conn.

Whitney Arms Co., New Haven, Conn. advertisement of August 15, 1878 *Forest and Stream.*

[117]

Chapter 24

PEABODY — MARTINI

The Peabody rifle mechanism was developed by Henry O. Peabody of Boston, Massachusetts, during the latter years of the American Civil War. The gun was presented to the Army Ordnance board and was tested and approved. The conclusion of the war cancelled all action, and the rifle was dropped from U.S. consideration.

Later a European by the name of Martini developed and improved certain aspects of the action. It was at this time that it became a hammerless action. The rifle was adopted by the Turkish, Egyptian, and English governments as a War Department issue rifle. The gun has been used throughout the world both for military and sporting purposes.

In the United States the rifle was made by the Providence Tool Company of Providence, Rhode Island.

The Providence Tool Company was organized in 1847 from a prior existing tool company and manufactured tools, sewing machines, industrial tools and rifled muskets for the United States. The Peabody rifles were also manufactured by this company.

In 1883 the Providence Tool Company went out of existence and was reorganized as the Rhode Island Tool Company.

The Peabody-Martini rifles continued to be manufactured in many foreign countries and many fine German and Swiss Schuetzen rifles have been made based on this action.

If you use breech seated bullets with this action you will find that it takes some ingenuity to make a breech seating tool that will work.

At the time of the great International Long Range Rifle Matches, Creedmoor rifles were made by the Providence Tool Company. These rifles are very well made and some are exceptionally fine guns.

The Creedmoor, Creedmoor Mid Range, Kill Deer, and the "What Cheer" models were all very finely made rifles.

The "What Cheer" model was named after the Providence rifle range which was just a few miles from the Providence Tool Company.

These fine guns were not popular with the American shooters and as a result not too many were made.

The August 15, 1878 issue of *Forest and Stream* reviewed the new Peabody Martini rifle for the benefit of the readers.

The "Kill Deer" pattern rifle was especially recommended for use on the plains for hunting big game.

The caliber recommended for 100 to 600 yard shooting was the .45 Government cartridge.

The match rifle was described as a "superb arm" which used 100 to 115 grains of powder with a 550 grain bullet in .44 caliber.

Providence Tool Co., Providence, Rhode Island advertisement for the Peabody-Martini match rifle, August 15, 1878 *Forest and Stream.*

Chapter 25

GERMAN EAGLE TARGET

Although one will find occasional illustrations of the German Eagle Target in the 1870 - 1900 sporting journals of the time, it is A. C. Gould who wrote the *Modern American Rifles* in 1892 that we have to thank for illustrating and giving detailed instructions for its construction and use.

The German-Swiss style of target used at the great 1850 - 1900 shooting festivals was a wood constructed target known as the "Eagle". This target was introduced into the United States and became a standard shooting festival target during the 1870's to 1914 period. There is no recorded use of this target after 1914 in the United States.

The target was 9 feet high and 12 feet wide. It was made up of 18 sections which were carefully doweled together. Each part was numbered and the shooter could only shoot at the part which was being fired at in the proper sequence. If the shooter knocked off another part he was penalized.

The parts were made of 1 inch pine wood and were held together with a ½ inch dowel. A dynamite cartridge was placed in the center of the body behind an 8 inch round iron plate with a ¾ inch hole in the center. When hit this exploded the body.

The whole assembly was placed on a 40 foot pole.

The sequence of shots took a long time for all entries could shoot until that particular part was off.

The scheduled sequence was as follows:

1. Ball of Center Crown.
2. Right small ball.
3. Left small ball.
4. Right flag.
5. Left flag.
6. Crown itself.
7. Right ring.
8. Left ring.
9. Reichsapfel
10. Sceptor.
11. Right head.
12. Left head.
13. Right shank.
14. Left shank.
15. Right wing.
16. Left wing.
17. Tail.
18. Body.

Eagle Schuetzen Target as shown in *Modern American Rifles* **by A.C. Gould, Bradlee Whidden, Boston, Mass., 1892.**

Chapter 26

ITEMS OF INTEREST

BULLET LUBRICATORS

Early experimenters with cartridge rifles found that a lead bullet fired in a rifled barrel required some type of lubrication to avoid lead build up and erratic shooting. The patched ball of the muzzle loader rifle provided a lubrication of the ball and prevented the lead from being in contact with the metal of the bore. Very early experimenters with lubrication simply dipped the whole cartridge in a lubricant which was usually common tallow.

Richard S. Lawrence, who did a lot of work on the Jenning's rifle, is credited with developing the use of lubrication grooves in the cast lead bullets and in the use of tallow for a lubricant. This occurred somewhere around 1850.

Albert Ball, who developed the Lamson-Ball rifles made during the Civil War at Windsor, Vermont, built a bullet greasing or lubricating machine for Springfield Armory in 1864 or 1865. He was granted a patent for this on May 23, 1865.

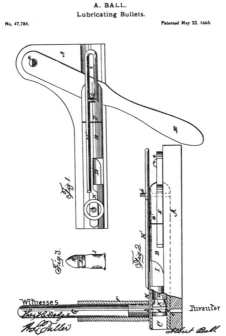

A. BALL.
Lubricating Bullets.

No. 47,784.

Patented May 23. 1865.

Patent Office. Patent issued to A. Ball May 23, 1865 - a device for lubricating bullets.

Mr. Ball adapted his machine to the use of power and made the mechanism into an automatic feed. The machine was used by cartridge factories both in the U.S. and abroad.

The Ideal Reloading Tool Company first came out with their No. 1 lubricator machine in 1899.

George C. Schoyen of Denver, Colorado and Harry M. Pope of Hartford, Connecticut both developed hand or bench type bronze lubricators of unique design for the lubrication of individual bullets cast by their molds.

H. M. Pope spent almost a year in Denver, Colorado in 1883. There are no clues as to what he did during this year. The similarities of the Schoyen and Pope bullet forms and the bullet lubricators are to great just to be dismissed as coincidence.

POWDER MEASURES

Shooting the muzzle loading rifles of the period prior to the introduction of the self contained cartridge required some type of a measure to insure regularity of the powder explosion and uniformity of discharge. In other words, to shoot a rifle at a known distance the powder charge must be consistant regardless of how it is measured.

When cartridge guns were developed, methods were devised to measure the powder charge which went into each case either initially or when the cartridge was reloaded. The basic principles were the same as used in powder measures today. The Ideal powder measure is simply a refinement of the number one measure of 1899.

One early measure had an adjustable chamber to permit varying the charge. This chamber was contained within a circular drum which could be rotated by a handle.

This measure was developed and patented by O. E. Michaelis, February 13, 1883. Michaelis was a Captain in the Ordnance Department stationed at Philadelphia, Pennsylvania.

The statement which he attached to the letter of application for a patent states, "My present invention relates to adjustable measures, such as are ordinarily used for measuring powder, shot, and similar materials; and the invention consists in a novel construction of the device, whereby it is rendered capable of being adjusted for different quantities with great accuracy, and is also capable of very fine adjustments or variations from its maximum to its minimum capacity..... ."

Captain Michaelis' powder measure looks and operates the same as those used today.

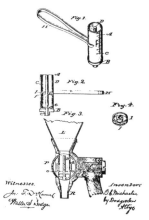

(No Model.)   O. E. MICHAELIS.
ADJUSTABLE POWDER CHARGER.
No. 272,072.   Patented Feb. 13, 1883.

Patent #272072 issued to O. E. Michaelis February 13, 1883 - adjustable powder measure. Note the revolving drum.

RODERICK BULLET LUBRICANT FORMULA

The following information was sent to me by Claude E. Roderick prior to his death at Monett, Missouri. Mr. Roderick had developed these formulas after much trial and error. The formulas have been used by a number of successful single shot riflemen in the midwest.

Mixtures for

RODERICK'S BULLET LUBRICANT FORMULAS

FORMULA No. 1

(HARD for use when weather temperature is 80° F. and above)
Approx. ½ lb. mixture:

50% Pure Beeswax	4 ozs.
40% Pure Mutton Tallow	3⅛ ozs.
10% Mobil 600W Steam Cylinder Oil	⅞ oz.

FORMULA No. 2

(MEDIUM for use when weather temperature is 55 to 80° F.)
Approx. ½ lb. mixture:

40% Pure Beeswax	3⅛ ozs.
50% Pure Mutton Tallow	4 ozs.
10% Mobil 600W Steam Cylinder Oil	⅞ oz.

FORMULA No. 3

(SOFT for use when weather temperature is below 55° F.)
Approx. ½ lb. mixture:

30% Pure Beeswax	2½ ozs.
60% Pure Mutton Tallow	4⅞ ozs.
10% Mobil 600W Steam Cylinder Oil	⅞ oz.

Avoid mixing too large a batch at a time. A ½ pound mixture is a two year supply for the average shooter. Keep it in air tight storage at all times.

Prepare the mixture in a couple of tin cans, one inside the other, and the outer one filled about one-third with water. Melt the beeswax first and when it is fully melted put in the tallow and cylinder oil stirring thoroughly, and KEEP ON STIRRING in the inner can until lubricant is chilled under cold water, or in ice water in the outer container. This is to keep heavier ingredients from settling to the bottom.

Shoot freshly lubricated bullets — not over two weeks old; then only if they have been kept wrapped up air tight. Shooting freshly lubricated bullets, and using ANY lube mixture at the temperature that it was compounded for, is a *MUST*! I have seen this fact demonstrated many times on our local range. If your bullets have the harder lube on them they can usually be used in a cooler temperature by putting softer lube on them with a grease pump or uniformly smearing the softer lube on with your fingers. If you use the pie pan method of lubricating your bullets, wrap air tight and leave them in the pan until ready to use.

When a GOOD LOAD and BULLETS suddenly starts to flying wild, stop and "mine" your lead in the bore with a real good cleaning, or mercury treatment. Note what lube you are using on the bullets and the weather temperature. Lube on bullets should feel soft and a little tacky to the touch. You can get by fairly well by using soft lube in warmer temperatures but don't try to use hard lube in colder temperatures. *DON'T* underestimate the *IMPORTANCE* of fitting a lube mixture (ANY lube mixture) to the temp.

To fill my grease pumps, I put a bullet in the die and take a small amount of lube in a can and melt, stir, and then pour it into the pump—this avoids getting air in pump.

Appendix A

LOADS FOR SAFE SINGLE SHOT RIFLES

Although loadings have been given for powders which are no longer sold commercially, there is not much point in it; so I shall give only those loadings for which powders are available, and the powders are very limited. Hercules #2400 and Unique are still available, and Dupont #4227 and #4198 can also be used. A number of shooters are still using #4759, and it is the standard for most shooters. However, #4227 works equally well, but NOT in the same loadings as #4759.

In duplex loading of all calibers use not more than 10% of the total charge as a primer charge of smokeless and fill the rest of the case with black powder; i.e., .32/40. 10% of 40 is 4 grains bulk; (set the Ideal measure on 4 grains — this is BULK measure) use Dupont IMR 4227 or 4198; fill the rest of the case with a second measure set to throw the bulk measure of black powder. FFG is the most suitable granulation, although FFFG will be found more desirable in the .25 and .22 calibers. Adjust the smokeless loading to give clean shooting, but only with careful experimentation, for smokeless loadings will increase pressures.

All loadings are for rifles of known or tested safety. The mold numbers shown are the old original Ideal numbers.

(Note: all powder weights are weighed amounts)

.22 Maynard (originally made for 10 gr. black powder)	228151		3.4 grs. Unique
.22 WCF	228151	45 gr.	3.6 grs.
.25/20/86 Stevens, Win., Rem. and other arms. Stevens and Maynard do best with 86 gr. bullet; Win. with 65-70 gr. bullet	257283	85 gr.	5.0 grs. Unique
	Same	86 gr.	8.0 grs. Herc. #2400
	25719	73 gr.	4.0 grs.
.25/21/86 and .25/25/86 Same loading as above but experimentation may prove that slightly heavier loads may be desirable, but increase with caution.			Unique

.28/30/120	285271	120 gr.	11.0 grs. #4227
	285222	120 gr.	11.0 grs. #4227
.32 Ideal	32359	115 gr.	4.0 grs. Unique
	32360	75 to 225 gr.	7.0 grs. #4227
.32/20 WCF	31133	110 gr.	10.0 grs. #2400
	31133	110 gr.	5.5 grs. Unique
	3118	115 gr.	5.5 grs. Unique or 9.5 grs. #4227
.32/30 Rem.	31326	98 gr.	7.0 grs. #4227
.32/35 Stevens & Maynard	3114	75 to 225 gr.	12.0 grs. #4227
.32/40 Bullard	3114	75 to 225 gr.	12.0 to 14.0 grs. #4227
.32/40 Remington	30812	80 to 201 gr.	Same as .32/40
.32/40 Ballard, Win., Marlin	31949	82 to 205 gr.	11.0 grs. #2400
	319289	185 gr.	11.0 grs. #2400
	319289	185 gr.	13.0 grs. #4227
	319247	165 gr.	12.0 grs. #2400
	32360	125 gr.	13.0 grs. #2400

Dr. Hudson Schuetzen bullet	319273	185 gr.	11.0 grs. #2400
	319273	185 gr.	13.0 grs. #4227
	321247	155 gr.	13.6 grs. #2400
.33/47 Pope & Schoyen	Lead	200 gr.	14.5 grs. #4227
.38/55 Ballard, Win., Marlin	37583	149 gr.	5.0 grs. Unique
	375248	250 gr.	15.0 grs. #2400
	375248	250 gr.	10.6 grs. Unique
Cork Wad	375248	250 gr.	18.0 grs. #4198
Instead of a wad some are using weighed kapok; old time shooters used Cream of Wheat.			or 18.1 grs. #4227
.40/70 Ballard or Sharps	403149	330 gr.	15.0 to 17 grs. #4227
	403149	330 gr.	22.5 gr. #4759
.45/70	Lead	405 gr.	22.0 gr. #4759
.45/90	Lead	310 gr.	17.0 gr. #4759

Appendix B

SELECTED SOURCE MATERIALS

AMERICAN FIELD, CHICAGO FIELD SPORTSMAN'S JOURNAL. Various issues covering period 1874 to 1888.
BAKER, LEIGHTON L. "Axel Peterson." Unpublished manucript. Colorado State Historical Society Library, Denver, Colorado.
BOSTON GLOBE. Boston Massachusetts. "William Malcolm." p. 15, March 10, 1913.
CLEDE, BILL. "Marlin Practical Gunmaker." *Shooting Times,* Peoria, Illinois. p. 8, March, 1963. P. 11, April, 1963.
COLORADO STATE HISTORICAL SOCIETY LIBRARY. Carlos Grove. George Schoyen, John Lower, Axel Peterson. Clippings, pictures, news articles, and archives of Colorado State Historical Society Library, Denver, Colorado.
DENVER PUBLIC LIBRARY. Western History Division, Denver, Colorado.
DIXIE GUNWORKS, INC. Catalog #119 Union City, Tennessee.
DOWAGIAC DAILY NEWS. "Adolph Niedner." Dowagiac, Michigan. December 27, 1954.
E. REMINGTON & SONS. Catalogs 1877, 1882. Ilion, New York.
GUNSIGHT GUIDE. "Stevens Rifle Telescopes." Follett Publishing Company, Chicago, Illinois, 1968.
HATCH, ALDEN. *Remington Arms.* Rinehart & Company, Inc., New York, 1956.
IDEAL MFG CO. New Haven, Connecticut. Hand book and Catalog #7 1896.
J. STEVENS ARMS AND TOOL COMPANY. Chicopee Falls, Massachusetts. Catalogs 1888 to 1948.
KELVER, GERALD. *Major Ned H. Roberts and the Schuetzen Rifle.* Mentone Press, Mentone, Indiana, 1951.
KIMBALL, W. G. C. "The Chicopee Falls Rifle." *American Rifleman.* p. 43, September, 1948.
LUSTYIK, ANDREW F. "The Lamson Company Carbines." *Gun Report.* Aledo, Illinois. July, August 1966.
MARLIN FIREARMS COMPANY. *Marlin Firearms 1870-1950. Marlin Gunzette.* New Haven, Connecticut.
MASSACHUSETTS ARMS COMPANY. Chicopee Falls, Massachusetts. Catalog 1880.
MODERN AMERICAN RIFLES. Bradlee Whidden, Boston, Massachusetts, 1892.
SATTERLEE, L.O. *10 Old Gun Catalogs. 14 Old Gun Catalogs.* Gun Digest Association, Inc., Chicago, Illinois.

SCOFIELD, JOHN. "The Old Master." *American Rifleman. p. 5, June, 1941.*

SELL, DE WITT. "Chicopee Falls - end of an era." p. 92, Gun Digest, 1965. Follett Publishing Company, Chicago, Illinois.

SELLERS, FRANK. *Stevens Firearms History. George Freund.* Unpublished research materials. Denver, Colorado.

SERVEN, JAMES E. "A.O. Zischang." *American Rifleman. p. 34, January, 1950.*

SHARPE, PHILIP B. The Rifle in America. William Morrow & Co., New York, 1938.

SHARPS RIFLE COMPANY. Original materials. Frank Sellers, Denver, Colorado.

SMITH, RAY M. *The Story of Pope's Barrels.* Stackpole Company, Harrisburg, Pennsylvania, 1960.

SYRACUSE PUBLIC LIBRARY. Obituary, William O. Zischang. Syracuse, New York.

WHELEN, MAJOR TOWNSEND. *The American Rifle.* The Century Co., New York, 1918.

WINCHESTER RPTG. ARMS CO. New Haven, Connecticut. Catalogs 1893-1916.

WINGATE, GENERAL GEORGE W. "Recollections of the National Rifle Association." *American Rifleman.* p. 32, May, 1941. p. 39, June, 1942.

WORCHESTER FREE LIBRARY. "H. Charles Ballard." Clippings, archives, Social Science Division, Worcester Free Library, Worcester, Massachusetts.